Women and Public Theology

Women and Public Theology

Emerging Voices

Edited by Elissa Cutter
and Allison Murray

Paulist Press
New York / Mahwah, NJ

Scripture quotations are from New Revised Standard Version Bible: Catholic Edition, copyright © 1989, 1993 National Council of the Churches of Christ in the United States of America. Used by permission. All rights reserved worldwide.

Cover image by AliMansoor / Shutterstock.com
Cover design by Sharyn Banks
Book design by Lynn Else

Copyright © 2024 by Elissa Cutter and Allison Murray

All rights reserved. No part of this publication may be reproduced, stored in a retrieval system, or transmitted in any form or by any means, electronic, mechanical, photocopying, recording, scanning, or otherwise, without either the prior written permission of the Publisher, or authorization through payment of the appropriate per-copy fee to the Copyright Clearance Center, Inc., www.copyright.com. Requests to the Publisher for permission should be addressed to the Permissions Department, Paulist Press, permissions@paulistpress.com.

Library of Congress Cataloging-in-Publication Data
Names: Cutter, Elissa, editor.
Title: Women and public theology: emerging voices / edited by Elissa Cutter and Allison Murray.
Description: Paperback. | New York; Mahwah, NJ: Paulist Press, [2024] | Summary: "A collection of essays adapted from blog entries on WIT: Women in Theology"—Provided by publisher.
Identifiers: LCCN 2023039852 (print) | LCCN 2023039853 (ebook) | ISBN 9780809156108 (paperback) | ISBN 9780809187706 (ebook)
Subjects: LCSH: Feminist theology. | Women theologians. | Theologians.
Classification: LCC BT83.55 .W63 2024 (print) | LCC BT83.55 (ebook) | DDC 230.082—dc23/eng/20240213
LC record available at https://lccn.loc.gov/2023039852
LC ebook record available at https://lccn.loc.gov/2023039853

ISBN 978-0-8091-5610-8 (paperback)
ISBN 978-0-8091-8770-6 (e-book)

Published by Paulist Press
997 Macarthur Boulevard
Mahwah, NJ 07430
www.paulistpress.com

Printed and bound in the
United States of America

Dedicated with gratitude to the women in theology
who broke the stained glass ceiling before us and
to those who encouraged us to join in the work.

CONTENTS

Preface: Women and Public Theology ix
    Elissa Cutter and Allison Murray

About *WIT: Women in Theology* xvii

1. Public Theology Matters 1
    Maria Gwyn McDowell

PART 1: APPROACHING THEOLOGY

2. Becoming a Feminist Theologian: On Doing Gender in the Theological Academy 13
    Brandy Daniels

3. Still Not Reading Barth 28
    Janice McRandal

4. *Théologienne, Théologien,* Theologian? Feminist Historical Theology from Angélique Arnauld to Mary Daly 38
    Elissa Cutter

5. Unpacking "Biblical Womanhood": Theological Nostalgia, Gender, and History 57
    Allison Murray

6. God of My Ancestors: A Filipina American Catholic's Reflection on Decolonizing Her Faith 70
    Jessica Gapasin Dennis

Contents

PART 2: PRACTICING THEOLOGY
7. For Whom Are We Outraged? 95
   Maria Gwyn McDowell

8. Unholy Trinity: Incel Ideology, Complementarian
   Theology, and Toxic Masculinity 109
   Alexandria Barbera and Allison Murray

9. Discerning the "Signs of the Times" and Doing Public
   Theology in an Evangelical Context 125
   Mandy Rodgers-Gates

10. The Religious Significance of Anorexia 140
    Caroline Morris

11. "Two Strikes": Or Why I Write for *Women in Theology* 154
    Jane Barter

Contributors 167

◇◇◇◇◇
PREFACE
Women and Public Theology
Elissa Cutter and Allison Murray

> Theology is a place and a story. Theology is the place and the story you think of when you ask yourself about the meaning of your life, of the world, of the possibility of God.
>
> Serene Jones, *Call It Grace: Finding Meaning in a Fractured World* (2020)

Where can women have a place to tell their stories of theology? In 2010, a group of graduate students at the University of Notre Dame—seeking such a place for themselves—decided to create a communal place where they could write publicly about their theological ideas, and thus *WIT: Women in Theology* (https://womenintheology.org/) came into existence. In the over ten years since its inauguration, *WIT* has expanded and developed into a popular shared blog, written by a community of women trained in the academic discipline of theology. Although other shared theological blogs exist, this one remains unique as an ecumenical place for scholars and writers of theology. Our contributors have spiritual and academic ties to Catholic, Eastern Orthodox, and Protestant traditions. We include a variety of methodological perspectives as well—systematic, historical, ethical, pastoral, and so on—within a shared commitment to the social, political, economic, domestic, and ecclesiastical equality of women. The community aspect of *WIT* is especially important because it allows for an ongoing conversation—between *WIT* and other theological blogs and even among the *WIT* authors themselves. Two of the contributions to this volume—those by Brandy Daniels and Janice McRandal—originated out of this type of ongoing conversation in a series of blog posts. In these public conversations, *WIT*'s contributors and readers come from around the English-speaking world.

Although all the regular contributors at *WIT* have a background in academic theology, the blog allows us to apply our academic training to speak to a public and popular audience. *WIT* does not just do feminist theology in this sense, but rather contemporary public feminist theology for issues that deserve an academic perspective. Although public theology has a multiplicity of meanings, the work of *WIT* resonates with the definition of Ted Peters as theology that "is conceived in the church, reflected on critically in the academy, and meshed within the wider culture for the benefit of the wider culture."[1] The women of *WIT* are all academically trained in theology and working from within Christian faith traditions to put theology into dialogue with culture and politics. *WIT* thus provides a space for women's voices to speak credibly to contemporary issues. Unfortunately, providing a space for women to speak authoritatively in the public sphere comes with a risk and many of the comments on some of our more controversial posts provide some evidence of this. Commenters will dismiss the intellectual argument put forward in posts and instead attack us in our identity as authors or theologians and our ability to write. For example, a comment on one of the posts by Katie Grimes, one of the original contributors to the blog, told her that she should "check you [sic] feminist privilege." Another commenter went back to a previous post in which she provided a theological analysis of Tupac Shakur—as theology and popular culture is a topic frequently addressed on the blog—and concluded that her praise of the theology underlying his work "tells us first and foremost that in your chosen career you are not to be taken seriously." Katie Grimes is an ethicist by training and so frequently wrote posts about topics that drew sustained attention, but she is by no means the only author to draw the ire of the public for daring to speak publicly as a woman in theology. In fact, the very boldness of *WIT* comes from its existence—women writing publicly about theology represents, to some readers, a crisis of authority, something that our pursuit of academic credentials and a deeper level of inquiry cannot seem to overcome, as Elissa Cutter addresses in her contribution to this volume.

Despite the risk that comes for women doing public theology, the original founders of *WIT* started the blog to create a place to do and publicize feminist theology. Like many theology departments across the country, although women had a presence as faculty and graduate students at Notre Dame, the founders found a lack of spaces for speaking about feminist theological issues. Elizabeth Antus, one of the founders, described their situation as feeling "starved for feminist theological conversation." As a result of this, they made requests to the faculty to have the doctoral curriculum changed so there would be a seminar on feminist theology taught in regular rotation. They also came together to start the blog because at the time more theologians were starting intellectually oriented blogs, but the founders found that it was mainly male scholars participating in the blogosphere and these new blogs were not addressing feminist issues. The founders found inspiration in the women scholars who had served as mentors and inspirations to them during their graduate and undergraduate studies. Decades prior, these women had a group that called themselves "WIT" when they had been in graduate school. This group—like others in existence in departments of theology around the country—provided support and community for women in an academic field that remains dominated by men. In this way, the blog *WIT: Women in Theology* represents a continuation and transformation of this tradition, bringing women's voices out of their communal gatherings and into the public sphere. In doing so, *WIT* provides a challenge to the culture of patriarchy in both the church and the secular world. *WIT* thus aims to fulfill the goals of feminist public theology expressed by Rosemary Carbine, namely "not to incorporate some marginalized women and men into an existing patriarchal body politic but to contest and change that body politic itself. In other words, feminist rhetorical space and its practices accent solidarity and social-political change rather than consensus."[2]

We are a new generation of women theologians, establishing our voices and speaking out publicly about theology and contemporary injustices. We do public theology as a form of protest—a means of raising our voices and drawing attention to important issues facing women and the church today. The popular nature of the blog allows more freedom to do this than traditional academic discourse in some ways. The nature of *WIT* as public theology provides a platform that legitimizes the anger that should face injustices in the world. By doing so, we are reforming the nature of what "counts" as theological discourse. In the context of *WIT*, we do not see a problem with allowing our emotion to show in our writing. It is an illusion to think that unemotional is the same as objective. Rather, especially when faced with injustices, emotion—anger—is precisely what is called for.[3] Our writing in this way challenges the nature of academic theological discourse in the same way that the idea of experience as a theological source has done in earlier feminist and liberation types of theology. Just as all theologians allow their experience to influence their interpretation of theological sources, so too with emotion. By permitting emotion, we challenge the misogynistic stereotype that says only women are emotional. Women are emotional, but so are men—or they should be—and our emotion can be a powerful motivation both for our theology and to address issues of injustice.[4]

Our work similarly shifts theological discourse by challenging the distinction between theology and spirituality. In the broad realm of theological studies, scholars of Christian spirituality define their discipline as the study of the Christian experience precisely as experience.[5] Spirituality, in this sense, is at least partly distinct from theology, which focuses on ideas, concepts, and doctrine—not the human experience of those things.[6] Often, when women write on themes of Christian thought and practice, their work gets categorized as "spiritual" rather than "theological."[7] Generally, this appears to happen as women's writings are considered to be interesting or applicable only to women readers; because the ideas offered come from reflections on specific experiences; or because the writings offer insight into problems or situations that are context dependent. The attention paid to social location in women's writings designates such work as "spirituality," instead of "theology." Given the pejorative roots of the term *spirituality* in seventeenth-century France, as a negative term applied to interior religious experience, the use of the term today for women's writings may retain some of that negative judgment as opposed to the "rational" nature of theology.[8] In the contemporary context, theology as a discipline has connections to the academy—though some of the chapters in this book rethink this

Preface

restriction of the theological to the academic—whereas anyone can have a spirituality.[9]

At *WIT*, just as we consider the division of sources of theological reflection into "traditional" (i.e., legitimate) and "alternative" (i.e., illegitimate) categories of limited use, we consider the division between spirituality and theology to be a product of a hierarchical, male-dominated classification that gives more prestige and authority to ideas divorced from context and practice. To translate the feminist truism—the personal is political—to our context, we would say that the spiritual *is* theological. Maintaining a rigid distinction between these two spheres does not serve the greater theological task—in fact, it undermines it by perpetuating the idea that there is such a thing as noncontextual theology. Our experiences of the world necessarily influence our mode of thinking, whether we want to admit so or not.[10] Like other dualisms that have had a profound impact on Christian thought and practice throughout Christian history (soul/body, head/heart, grace/nature, church/world, etc.) the perpetuation of a hierarchical distinction between the theological and the spiritual has had the corollary impact of perpetuating the dismissal of women's voices as theologically authoritative. Contributors to this volume have all been trained in the theological academy, yet their approaches to their work sometimes contest the traditional practices and divisions of that academic space.

The essays in this volume both address the issue of theological method and aim to legitimize anger at social injustices. The contributors are all past or current regular contributors to the blog who have either revised and expanded blog posts they published in the past or written entirely new essays that relate to the methods, themes, and mission of *WIT*. Part 1, "Approaching Theology," includes contributions that raise questions about women's theological method and voices. The section begins with a reflection around two autoethnographic vignettes by Brandy Daniels about her experiences as a doctoral student, beginning a new career in theology. Analyzing her experiences alongside Judith Butler's theory of gender performativity, she traces the ways gender is still policed in the theological academy and highlights the importance of feminist spaces as resources for women in this context. This is followed by a piece by Janice McRandal that challenges the idea of academic canons that continue to perpetuate the overrepresentation of men, especially in systematic theology and studies of Karl Barth.

The next two chapters turn to questions about the relationship between history and theology. First, Elissa Cutter draws on the work of feminist theologians, the methods of historical theology, and the example of the seventeenth century "Jansenist" nuns of Port-Royal to explore the idea of feminist historical theology. Her chapter asserts the need for women to claim the title of theologian for themselves. Next, Allison Murray addresses questions about historical literacy as a necessary component of theological reflection. Focusing on the American evangelical concept of biblical womanhood, she analyzes the impact of ahistorical nostalgia within this version of theological anthropology, demonstrating that views about the direction of history play as central a role in the formation of "biblical womanhood" as engagement with scriptural texts (if not more).

The final chapter in this section explores theology specifically for women in an American context. Raising questions of intersectionality in relation to feminist theology, Jessica Gapasin Dennis examines her identity as a Filipina American Catholic in relation to the history of colonization. She proposes the idea of anamnesis as a means to make meaning out of history, by remembering and retelling stories that raise up our identities as children and image-bearers of God.

Part 2 of this volume, "Practicing Theology," includes contributions that address contemporary issues facing women in society and the church from a theological perspective. Maria McDowell opens this section with a reflection on the role of anger and outrage as we engage in the work of social transformation and justice making. Focusing on outrage as an initiation mechanism, she argues that our outrage must move us toward questions of responsibility and accountability. Encouraging us to see connections between contemporary outrage-evoking events and historical patterns of injustice that laid the foundation of these events, this contribution places anger and social transformation within a mutually supportive framework.

Outrage and anger also play a role in Alexandria Barbera and Allison Murray's coauthored piece on toxic masculinity. Anchoring their reflections on the 2018 Toronto Van Attack, they explore uncomfortable parallels between "incel" rhetoric and assumptions embedded within evangelical complementarian theology. Focusing specifically on how these two seemingly disparate groups view women's roles in men's lives, this chapter argues that toxic notions about masculinity show a permeable boundary between the religious and the secular.

Mandy Rogers-Gates contributes a proposal for the role of public theology within American evangelicalism as a response to Christian nationalism. Arguing that additional attention to structural sin is needed, she draws on insights from the Latin American church while proposing an evangelical version of public theology that accounts for both message and context to be taken seriously. Expectations regarding women's bodies are the focus of the final chapter in this section, Caroline Morris's essay on anorexia. As she works to provide a theological reclamation of appetite—something long denied or held in suspicion within the Christian tradition—she argues for the importance of appetite-as-virtue and highlights the problems that arise in communities of faith that emphasize control over pleasure.

These two parts to our text are framed by two essays that began as part of a series that many of our contributors participated in over the summer of 2019 about why they write for *WIT*. The first essay from this series, by Maria McDowell, addresses the importance of *WIT* as a platform for women doing public theology, both by circumventing the tacit silencing of dissenting voices—especially those of women—and allowing for a collaborative and communal model for doing theology. Our concluding essay is Jane Barter's piece from this series, which provides a reflection on the marginalization of theology and feminism in the study of religion, arguing for the importance of theology despite these experiences.

As we mark and celebrate more than a decade of women doing public theology as part of *WIT*, we are grateful for earlier feminist disruptions in theology that made a space in which *WIT* could emerge. We hope our work will continue to make space for other marginalized or "nontraditional" approaches to (and voices in) theology to be heard, considered, and engaged in the decades to come.

Notes

1. Ted Peters, "Public Theology: Its Pastoral, Apologetic, Scientific, Political, and Prophetic Tasks," *International Journal of Public Theology* 12 (2018): 155.

2. Rosemary P. Carbine, "Ekklesial Work: Toward a Feminist Public Theology," *The Harvard Theological Review* 99, no. 4 (2006): 450.

3. Elizabeth Antus, "Joining the 'Symphony of Anger': Reflecting the Pressure for an Apologetics of Rage," American Academy of Religion Annual Meeting, San Diego, California, November 23–26, 2019.

4. On the importance of anger as an emotion and the means of developing virtuous anger derived from Thomas Aquinas and scientific data, see William Mattison, "Virtuous Anger? From Questions of *Vindicatio* to the Habituation of Emotion," *Journal of the Society of Christian Ethics* 24, no. 1 (2004): 159–79.

5. See, for example, Lawrence S. Cunningham and Keith J. Egan, *Christian Spirituality: Themes from the Tradition* (Mahwah, NJ: Paulist Press 1996), 2, 7–9, and Michael Downey, *Understanding Christian Spirituality* (Mahwah, NJ: Paulist Press, 1997), 8, 14, 91.

6. For the connections between theology and spirituality, see Cunningham and Egan, *Christian Spirituality*, 25–26, and Downey, *Understanding Christian Spirituality*, 145–6, 149.

7. For critiques of this tradition, see Andrew Prevot, "No Mere Spirituality: Recovering a Tradition of Women Theologians," *Journal of Feminist Studies in Religion* 33, no. 1 (2007): 107–17 and Elissa Cutter, "No Church Mothers: Part III, Theology vs. Spirituality," *WIT: Women in Theology*, May 10, 2022, https://womenintheology.org/2022/05/10/no-church-mothers-part-iii-theology-vs-spirituality/.

8. See Cunningham and Egan, *Christian Spirituality*, 5.

9. Downey, *Understanding Christian Spirituality*, 31.

10. Downey, *Understanding Christian Spirituality*, 48.

ABOUT *WIT:* WOMEN IN THEOLOGY

WIT: Women in Theology is a shared blog by women trained in the academic disciplines of theology who write from a Christian ecumenical and often feminist perspective. Our group includes scholars and writers who have spiritual and academic ties to Eastern Orthodox, Protestant, and Catholic traditions, and we are committed to ecumenical collaboration. We hope that our diverse theological perspectives and many ways of naming our commitment to the social, political, economic, domestic, and ecclesiastical equality of women can emerge through this collaboration. On *WIT* we focus our academic training on a wide variety of topics, reflecting our shared commitment to the flourishing of women. For more on *WIT*, see https://womenintheology.org/about/.

WIT's regular contributors commit to writing a minimum of four posts each calendar year. The blog is managed by an executive board of up to five regular contributors, two of whom serve as editors. *WIT* also invites specific women to write guest posts on topics related to current events and relevant theological conversations. These posts deeply enrich the content of *WIT*. If you are interested in contributing to the blog, or would like more information about our contributors, see https://womenintheology.org/contributing/.

1
PUBLIC THEOLOGY MATTERS

Maria Gwyn McDowell

I joined *Women in Theology* (*WIT*) in 2013 after writing as an Eastern Orthodox feminist on my personal blog, *DeiProfundis*. I applied for two related reasons. First, in Eastern Orthodoxy, silence and isolation is a tool to quell dissent. Second, and related, there were simply no public and collaborative venues for the discussion of Orthodox theology in a feminist and liberationist vein. I am no longer Orthodox, but I still write for *WIT* because my underlying conviction, the conviction that drove me to pursue a PhD in theological ethics in the first place, remains: collaborative public theology matters.[1]

The essays collected in this book span a variety of perspectives, disciplines, and voices, from theologians who identify as women. They represent a form of collaborative public theology that arises out of the concerns and questions of particular women in particular times and places, shaped by personal experiences, passions, and convictions, and richly sourced from a well of rigorous intellectual engagement. The authors have a variety of reasons they write for *WIT*, but a roundtable series on why we joined highlighted common threads: the desire to engage as a woman, with other women, in a collaborative theological conversation in a field dominated by men.[2]

Women and Public Theology

Silencing Dissent

By 2013, I had completed my PhD in theological ethics, and realized in the three years since that (1) no Orthodox institution would ever hire a woman who wrote about ordaining women to the sacramental priesthood, and (2) no non-Orthodox institution knew what to do with a feminist, liberationist, Eastern Orthodox woman. There was no niche in which I fit, at least, not a niche that offered legitimate employment. I had no clear place in which to advocate for what I cared about most: the full dignity of women in Orthodoxy, and the ethical necessity of recognizing their full participation in the sacramental priesthood.

When I spoke about the ordination of women to the Orthodox priesthood, whether on my blog, in churches, or classrooms, I was regularly told, "No one shares your opinion, you should go be an Episcopalian." For too many Orthodox, this is simply an indirect way of calling someone a heretic (someone who is incorrect regarding church doctrine), or even apostate (someone who understands and explicitly rejects church doctrine). In Orthodox conferences where women in ministry was the topic, I was rarely invited to contribute, unless, ironically, the conference was organized by non-Orthodox. I was once in a plenary session given by a highly respected Orthodox theologian where I asked a question about women in the church. He responded, "You are currently the expert on this topic," did not address the question, and then went on to organize subsequent conversations on the topic, without ever proactively inviting me to contribute. "Safer" women, that is, women who did not discuss the sacramental priesthood, were invited.

The reality is that sympathetic male Orthodox theologians (and priests) are in a difficult position. They risk their reputations, and even their jobs, if they show public support. I knew I was not alone in my convictions, but the openly supportive group of colleagues with whom to substantively engage any question of women in the church that did not fall along "traditionalist" lines was very small. In Orthodoxy, a silent nonresponse, or, when forced, a dismissive silencing, is the norm. Open dissent, no matter how graciously delivered, is met with hostility.

Examples of this hostility abound. The Orthodox Theological Society in America recently addressed the topic of academic freedom precisely because academic theologians (who are often clergy) are regularly threatened by self-identified "traditionalist" groups with public shaming and ecclesiological punishment.[3] Bishops of clergy who address controversial (that is, anything deemed outside the exceedingly narrow bounds of what they define as "traditional") are challenged to silence or remove these theologians. Rod Dreher, a leading voice at *American Conservative* and a current darling of traditionalist Orthodox, condemns dialogue on subjects that raise questions regarding established church teaching and labels as dangerous liberals those who engage in open conversations.[4] Public Orthodoxy, seen as a bastion of "liberalism" by traditionalists such as Dreher, was one of nine hundred websites blocked in Russia.[5] The exchange between Dreher and defenders of dialogue such as the Rev. Dr. John Jillions or many of the authors at Public Orthodoxy may seem academic, but it has profound political impact. Metr. Kirill, Patriarch of Moscow, justified the invasion of Orthodox Ukraine by Orthodox Russia as a defense of traditional family values and against the Western imposition of Pride parades.[6] The hostility toward "untraditional" values is so intense that peaceful demonstrations are viewed as a legitimate excuse for violence.

When I applied to write for *WIT*, Public Orthodoxy did not yet exist. Conversations regarding female ordination and nonheteronormative relationships were limited to private Facebook groups and in-person gatherings. Writing for *WIT* was a way to make more public a conversation many had no idea was happening. One facet of the silencing of alternative views within Orthodoxy was the constant public assurance to Orthodox and non-Orthodox Christians that Orthodoxy would never change, and no "good" Orthodox was also a feminist. My goal was to publicly demonstrate that some Orthodox were indeed committed to the full dignity of women in the church, and the full recognition of their gifts and roles.

Good Theology Is Collaborative Theology

Working outside of the academy also meant that I was not in the kind of conversations that give me joy: my conversation partners were in other cities, and while I was a part of some truly amazing and thoughtful Facebook groups, they tended to be insular (and, safe, in a sometimes very necessary way). My best theology, by which I mean those theological pieces I have written that people tell me give them hope, make them think, and encourage them to persist, always came from a collaborative space.

Collaboration is often (though not always) a hallmark of feminist theological commitments. The *Journal of Feminist Studies in Religion* uses roundtable discussions to intentionally create conversation across perspectives and disciplines.[7] Efforts to collaborate often intentionally highlight voices typically left out of academic consensus: non-Western, nonwhite, and nonmale. The Cooperative, "a project in public collaboration in the spirit of public theology," founded by former *WIT* member Janice McRandal, notes in its value statement that "the historic idea of a *public* is based on the inclusion of a small group of men" and so commits itself to only staging "conversations that are broad and inclusive."[8]

I went to graduate school not because I love academic study (I am certainly partial to it), but because I think theology matters. What we believe matters because it affects what we do and how we are in the world. Too often, people think theology is a remote discipline. This is an understandable mistake since so many theologians converse primarily among themselves. Conversation sharpens our thought, reminds us of those we have neglected, offers metaphors and stories that deepen the impact of doctrine. *WIT* gave me an opportunity to engage in a more public conversation with women and men who shared my convictions, but not always my perspective.

Collaborative Theology Matters!

I was not content to only be in a supportive theological conversation within *WIT*, but I wanted a public conversation about something I considered essential. Conversations about what matters to us are too often buried in academic journals. We forget that one of the great controversies of the church was conducted via raucous singing in the streets of the (Byzantine) Roman empire as Arius and Athanasius wielded weapons of sung theology while arguing the created or uncreated nature of the Son. The question of who Jesus was—God, human, or some combination of both or neither—was not an abstract theological question bandied about by theologians and leaders of the church, and the need for a shared understanding was not simply about ensuring imperial conformity. Fourth-century Christians were processing in the streets, using hymns as theological weapons (some things never change). The priest Arius, who held that both the Son and Holy Spirit were not fully God, coined the ditty, "There was when he was not." What Arius meant by this is that there was a time when Jesus did not exist. In good debate form, his bishop Alexander injected a single word, and sent his own followers into the streets singing "there was *not* when he was not." With sailors in major port cities spreading theological controversy through song (apparently all protest movements sing!), the fragile peace of the newly united Roman Empire was at risk, and a theologically ambivalent Constantine ordered the Christians to settle their differences and calm down. While we can debate the invasion of the state into church at this point, what is clear is that people were passionate enough about theology that they were making trouble in the streets. Such passion is rarely generated by abstract ideas; it is generated when the very possibility of your relationship with God is in jeopardy.[9]

For a more contemporary example, consider Nadia Bolz-Weber's recent book *Shameless: A Sexual Reformation*.[10] It is an exceptionally good book. As someone who has studied sexual ethics for a while now, what she says isn't new to me. It isn't new to any academic specializing in sexual ethics. But Bolz-Weber's ability to take significant theological material and make it clear, accessible, and convicting is a gift many academically inclined theologians lack. I dream of being able to write like Bolz-Weber—a dream I will never realize because we have different kinds of theological gifts. What we share however, is the conviction that theology should matter to all of us and should be shared among all of us.

WIT was my opportunity to be a public, feminist, liberationist, Orthodox theologian. To freely write a theology that I hoped was life-giving not just for me, but other Orthodox, and for non-Orthodox.

The Vulnerability of Public Theology

Despite my eagerness for the opportunity to write for *WIT*, it was a fraught decision. My writing at *DeiProfundis*, and my academic work, arose out of my personal interests. Most of my posts there were about the ordination of women. What I had not publicly said was that by 2013, I was in love with a woman. My first *WIT* post, "Fragile Repentances," included examples from my immediate life, not just others (most, though, are from others).[11] The first line however, had been said to me two years before: "I can no longer offer you the Eucharist. While I cannot tell you to leave this parish, I would prefer you no longer attend." Despite this disinvitation, I continued attending liturgy but did not receive the Eucharist. It was one of the most awful periods of my life, standing in a church I loved knowing I was unwelcome. On Palm Sunday of 2013, a priest I had known since childhood went a step further: not only was I not to receive communion or attend the parish in which I was raised, I was told I was not welcome in any Orthodox parish in my hometown. People will tell you that only bishops can excommunicate you. But bishops abrogate this responsibility all the time, leaving such decisions to the "pastoral discernment" of their local priests. My wife and I were effectively excommunicated from the church that I loved. That I still love.

For me, it was the last straw. It was bad enough to stand in church, hear "God's Holy Gifts for God's Holy People" and know that I was not considered a member of that group. It was another to not be able to worship at all.

I left. We left. I reluctantly followed my wife to the Episcopal Church.

It was glorious. For the first time, I could worship without the rage and grief of being a woman called to the priesthood forced to watch only men live their calling. People loved my passion for theology and valued my ability to teach it with clarity, conviction, and humor. My gifts as a theologian and teacher were no longer a threat to less-educated clergy, but a welcome contribution to the community. I could hold my wife's hand. We could be married before God and our community! Hallelujah!!!!

As I wrote in "The Home That Joy Built," while I was excommunicated from Orthodoxy because I was partnered with a woman, I will never return because, finally, I am able to fully exercise my gifts and calling as a priest.[12]

I love being a priest. Truly, I love it. I don't love all the things that go into being the rector of a small, struggling parish. Seriously, who does? But I love that, finally, after years of struggling to acknowledge this call from God that would have been so much easier not to have, I get to be who God has called me to be: a priest in their church.

This shift in ecclesial homes and cultures makes writing a problem, in part because I just don't have time, but also because for so many years, my writing was fueled by a desire to help bring change to my beloved Orthodox community. But that community does not want me, and I am not sure I want to care about it anymore. That sounds harsh, but I am tired of fighting it and fighting for it. I feel like I have deserted my friends. Some of my friends think I have deserted them. But I am so tired. So tired that my dissertation, the only English-language book-length argument for the ordination of women to the sacramental priesthood from an Eastern Orthodox theological perspective (there is one in Greek), languishes in a Dropbox folder. In it, I engage Orthodox theologies of human personhood, liturgy, icons, and virtue ethics to argue that it is essential (and entirely consistent with doctrinal commitments) for Orthodoxy to recognize the unique and irreducible personhood of all people and their gifts, including the gifts of sacramental priesthood. The thing is, I am not sure who it is for anymore.

And my new community—it isn't that it is perfect, but it is so much…more peaceful. I am still getting to know it. The Episcopal Church is what I call "practice forward." It is willing to do what it thinks is right: to practice compassion, justice, and mercy, even if it does it clumsily or incompletely. I am so very grateful for its shelter. My presiding bishop, instead of issuing an "educational document" that shames trans folks based on an utterly imaginary view of gender complementarity, expressed gratitude for how LGBTQ siblings "help the church, not to build a bigger church for church's sake, but to build a better world for God's sake."[13]

As a priest, I am grateful every Sunday that I get to stand at God's table and welcome all those who are hungry for God to come and feast.

But it is strange being a priest in a culture that is not your own. (I have so many half-written blog posts about church as culture, about the romanticization of Eastern Orthodoxy by Western Christians, about the things that shouldn't be romanticized, and the things that really should be taken more seriously.) I am also the priest of a small, historically African American congregation. The only one in the Pacific Northwest. I am an Episcopalian from the Christian East, learning the culture of a deeply anglicized and Western church, leading a still-significantly African American congregation, in the whitest major city in the United States. My learning curve is steep. I live in a cultural maelstrom that I am not yet able to put into words.

But I will continue to write for *WIT*. Because women theologians, and priests, need a voice. Because silencing is the enemy of the work of God. Because theology matters, because it is best done in collaboration, and because it must be public.

May we never allow ourselves to remain silent.

NOTES

1. This essay is a revised and expanded version of the post "Why I Write for *WIT*: Collaborative Public Theology Matters," *WIT: Women in Theology*, June 13, 2019, https://womenintheology.org/2019/06/13/why-i-write-for-wit-collaborative-public-theology-matters/.

2. See "Category: Why I Write for *WIT*," *WIT: Women in Theology*, https://womenintheology.org/category/round-tables/why-i-write-for-wit/.

3. See the Church and the Academy Blog Project, https://www.otsamerica.net/the-church-and-the-academy-blog-project/.

4. See Dreher's Schmemann Lecture (Rod Dreher, "Living in Truth: How the Communist-Era Suffering Church Can Prepare Us to Be Dissidents," Voices of St. Vladimir's Seminary, February 10, 2021, https://podbay.fm/p/voices-from-st-vladimirs-seminary/e/1612990200) where he condemns dialogue, his critique of longtime defender of academic freedom and thoughtful dialogue Rev. Dr. John Jillions (Rod Dreher, "The Problem with 'Fundamentalists,'" *American Conservative*, February 1, 2022, https://www.theamericanconservative.com/dreher/john-jillions-orthodoxy-fundamentalists-dreher-hatfield/), and Jillions's response ("'The Master's Hospitality': Jesus and Dialogue," *Public Orthodoxy*, May 5, 2022, https://publicorthodoxy.org/2022/05/05/the-masters-hospitality-jesus-and-dialogue/).

5. Public Orthodoxy is at https://publicorthodoxy.org/.

6. See Sarah Riccardi-Schwarz, "In His 'Forgiveness Day' Sermon—a Slightly More Sophisticated 'Globohomo' Rant," *Religion Dispatches*, March 7, 2022, https://religiondispatches.org/in-his

-forgiveness-day-sermon-a-slightly-more-sophisticated-globohomo-rant-kirill-lays-out-an-authoritarian-vision-in-which-his-version-of-god-might-dominate-and-rule-the-h/.

7. See "Thirtieth-Anniversary Roundtable on JFSR" for a series of reflections on the importance of collaboration, *Journal of Feminist Studies in Religion*, Fall 2014.

8. See "About," *The Cooperative*, https://thecooperativehub.com/about/.

9. J. N. D. Kelly, *Early Christian Doctrines*, rev. ed. (San Francisco: HarperSanFrancisco, 1978), 227; Jonathan Hehn, "Congregational Song as Theological Debate in Late Antiquity: A Case Study of Arius's Thalia and the Development of Trinitarian Orthodoxy," *The Hymn* 65, no. 1 (2014): 13–20.

10. Nadia Bolz-Weber, *Shameless: A Sexual Reformation* (New York: Convergent Books, 2019).

11. See Maria Gwyn McDowell, "Fragile Repentances," *WIT: Women in Theology*, November 19, 2013, https://womenintheology.org/2013/11/19/fragile-repentances/.

12. Maria Gwyn McDowell, "The Home That Joy Built," in *The Church Has Left the Building*, ed. Michael Plekon, Maria Gwyn McDowell, and Elizabeth Schroeder (Eugene, OR: Cascade Books, 2016), 34–44.

13. See "Presiding Bishop's Pride Month Statement Honors LGBTQ Episcopalians," The Episcopal Church Office of Public Affairs, June 12, 2019, https://www.episcopalchurch.org/publicaffairs/presiding-bishops-pride-month-statement-honors-lgbtq-episcopalians/.

PART 1
APPROACHING THEOLOGY

2

BECOMING A FEMINIST THEOLOGIAN

On Doing Gender in the Theological Academy

Brandy Daniels

From Tertullian's claim that women are "a temple built over a sewer, the gateway to the devil" to Luther's assertion that the "words and works of God is quite clear, that women were made either to be wives or prostitutes"; from John Wesley's admonishments to his wife to be "content to be a private, insignificant person" to Paul Tillich's extra-marital affairs and womanizing tendencies—historically, Christian theologians have not exactly been known to be champions of women or of gender equality amid embodied difference.

Cultural norms around what, and thus who, counts as fully human, who is capable of intellectual inquiry, and what that means for the ordering of society from the family to the *polis* were long-drawn from male experience—from *particular* male experience, of those who have been afforded positions of privilege and power in accordance with not only gender/one's (presumed) genitalia, but also with one's race, ethnicity, class/socioeconomic status, and so on. These norms prevailed until those on the underside challenged them. Within Christian thought and practice, feminist theology—alongside Black and Latin American liberation theologies (among others)—has been a key avenue for this work, challenging theological claims of and bases for sexism and misogyny through a variety of methods, often through close readings and fresh interpretations of the very theologians whose sexist remarks it denounces.

In addition to the *doing* of feminist theology—that talk of God and of Christian beliefs and practices that takes seriously the perspective of women and pursues gender equality—much attention is given to the outcomes of the work of feminist theological reflection (that is, of what it has and has not yet accomplished) as well as to its methodology (that is, how it pursues the work). Much less attention, even in these methodological reflections, is given to the experiential elements of those who do the work itself. Even among those whose methodologies look to the lived experience of women as key sources for theological reflection, the focus is, understandably, on the lived experiences of those within the communities the theologian is speaking to or about. Given feminist theologies' aim to take seriously—to understand, critically interrogate, subvert and challenge—the ways in which power circulates across lines of gender and other forms of difference, and given the history of theological discourse regarding the status and voices (or lack thereof) of women, what might a turn to the lived experiences of those who do the work of feminist theological scholarship—to the social and material conditions of their lives, and attendant affective and phenomenological experiences—add to the conversation?

Exploring this question in depth is, admittedly (and unsurprisingly), beyond the scope of this brief chapter. While, again, there is a great deal of feminist theological scholarship that elevates and methodologically and constructively turns to women's experience, and while there is a plethora of research about the experiences of women in academia more broadly, there is more research and scholarship to be done—historically, ethnographically, qualitatively, theologically—at the intersection of these inquiries.[1] That being said, while there is certainly more to be done, there *have* been spaces that have explored and given voice to these intersecting inquiries—public scholarly spaces like the *Women in Theology* blog.

Becoming a Feminist Theologian

This chapter aims to highlight some ways in which *Women in Theology* has provided space for critical inquiry around and constructive changes for the lived experiences of women in theology. This chapter admittedly pursues that aim with a humble, limited scope—through a brief autoethnographic account, and subsequent theoretical/theological reflection, both of which were written as I was completing my doctoral coursework in Christian theological studies and initially appeared on the blog. My own experience is precisely and merely that, my own experience, but by placing it in conversation with feminist theory and theology, I explore some of the complex ways that norms, desire, and power converge around, with, and through gender in the theological academy, and in particular, identify and critically examine some of the double binds that women, as well as others who are a part of marginalized groups, face in the theological academy. Through situating those experiences within the context of the work of the *Women in Theology* blog, I also highlight how feminist theology might serve as a resource for navigating, subverting, and thriving in and amid spaces where sexism persists.

Background

I remember when I first came across the *Women in Theology* blog. I was in the last year of my master of divinity program and, at the encouragement of some of my professors, with much fear and trembling, was beginning to consider doctoral work in theological studies. I had fallen in love with theology and was doing well in my program, but often felt both lonely and a bit dazed, as a first-generation college student at a much-esteemed R1 divinity school, and, at the time, as one of only two out queer women in my program (the other being my then girlfriend). One of the lifelines at the time, in addition to a small handful of divinity professors who invested in and supported me, as well as the classes I was able to take in the literature program, was the then-booming "theo-blogosphere." In the late aughts, before social media transformed into what it is now (in the era where Facebook was used more for playing online games and posting "flair," pins that highlighted one's political proclivities and pop cultural interests on a virtual corkboard), and long before Substack, blogs thrived as a source and site for public intellectual conversations, and in the world of academic theology and philosophy of religion, they were especially popular.

Hosted and run by young theologians and philosophers, blogs like *An und für sich*, *Faith and Theology*, and *Die Evangelischen Theologen*, among others, not only produced ongoing theological content that kept pace with current events and theological trends and controversies at a speed that formal publications couldn't, but also served as sites for robust, and often contentious, theological discussions and debates.[2] I relished these sites and the conversations they engendered—it was a space where I could go at my own pace and contribute in a more anonymous format, where I could craft my contributions more carefully and wasn't so quickly overlooked because of perceptions of my gender, my class, or lack of academic bona fides. And it was a space that made theology feel even more alive, relevant, and exciting.

Over time, it was also a space that, in many ways, mimicked the isolating impact of the classroom. I could blend in more, yes, but I soon discovered that I really *had* to blend in, to argue in certain combative ways about particular metaphysical and theoretical topics, if I wanted to be taken seriously. Even then, my remarks were often overlooked among the plethora of comments and contentious exchanges. Most (all?) of the then prominent theology blogs were, to my recollection, challenging spaces for women to engage in. The material conditions and lived experiences of those participating in the conversations was often seen as a distraction to the discourse and debate at hand.[3] What started out for me as a balm became a kind of bludgeon. And then *Women in Theology* went live.

I distinctly remember when *Women in Theology* began in October of 2010. I had just sat down in my seat in Black Intellectuals and Religion, a class I was taking at the time with J. Kameron Carter—one of my favorite classes at the time—and my friend Matt turned around and asked if I'd heard about it. He mentioned that Carter had been mentioned in their initial post. I remember pulling up the blog during class, and wanting to both laugh and cry (in a good way). That initial post, by Julia, recounted Carter, following a talk he gave at the University of Notre Dame, offering some advice to a group of PhD students. At the heart of that advice was the importance of developing and embracing your own voice as a theologian. Julia went on to talk about the initial group that started *Women in Theology* taking that seriously, even if it meant the blog being slow to start given the group's other responsibilities.[4]

I had to stifle my simultaneous laughter and tears as Carter was lecturing on W. E. B. Dubois and Karl Barth because the content of that initial post hit *very* close to home. While Black Intellectuals and Religion was my favorite class, I was struggling in it. Not because I wasn't getting it, or connecting critically and constructively with the material, but because of precisely the opposite. I was connecting with the material a lot, but struggled to speak up, and every time I tried, a classmate would interrupt me or follow right after in a way that quickly moved the conversation past what I had to say. While there was a lot going into my struggle to find my voice, one detail that proved especially relevant was the gender makeup of the class. Out of over thirty students, only three of us were women. Just a week before Matt alerted me to this new blog, I'd had a particularly frustrating experience trying to speak, resulting in some tears. The following class, one of the other women in the class arrived with a gift for me. She fished around her backpack and pulled out a pink plastic water gun that was shaped like a penis and bedazzled and adorned with rainbow and unicorn stickers. Handing it to me, she simply said, "Now you have one too."

That gift of the pink plastic water gun, and the discovery of the then new *Women in Theology* blog and its initial post, marked a turning point for me, where I started to embrace and develop my own voice as a theologian, a process that *Women in Theology* not only helped catalyze but continued to facilitate as I continued to read and engage.[5] As another female blogger so aptly put it, "When *Women in Theology* started a number of years ago…it was like a breath of fresh air in a virtual space that tended to extend the old-boys-club atmosphere of theology rather than make space for other voices."[6] So two years later, when *Women in Theology* put out a call for contributors, I eagerly applied, and was invited to join their ranks.

I ended up contributing to *Women in Theology* for nearly two years, during which I wrote sixteen posts. My posts covered topics ranging from rape culture and pornography to shame and queerness to loneliness and belonging. Across the various topics I wrote on, themes of power, norms, or desire, and particularly how they were entangled with and through gender and sexuality, were consistent. Moreover, almost all my posts in some way drew on my own experiences, usually explicitly so. Blogging on *Women in Theology* offered me a way to both theologically and theoretically work through my own experiences, and in doing so, to use my own experiences as a resource for theological reflection. While these themes and trends were consistent throughout my posts, at times I was a bit more explicit in my engagement....

Manly Me (Theology Edition)

In the summer of 2013, author and essayist Rebecca Scherm wrote a piece for *The Hairpin* about her time interning at a men's magazine.[7] A friend with whom I had been watching the then popular show *Mad Men* sent it to me—the subject line of her email read "Mad Men, modern edition?" Yet when I read the essay, it reminded me less of a spin on *Mad Men* and more of a journalistic spin on my own experience in graduate school—as in, I felt like I could have just changed a few details, substituting "men's magazine," with "theological studies," and written basically the same thing (though with admittedly less eloquence). So with Scherm's permission, I did precisely that, posting my re-creation, on *Women in Theology*. I followed her format and often quoted her verbatim—both because I could not come up with more apt or eloquent words, and, importantly, to demonstrate the pervasiveness of the "Good Ol' Boys' club" across different contexts.[8] The following is an abbreviated and slightly edited version of my original post:

When I was twenty-six, I started really getting serious about the possibility of pursuing a PhD in theology, about pursuing a career in the field I flirted with in college and fell in love with in divinity school. One of my first strategic moves in this regard was to attend the main academic conference of the guild, the annual meeting of the American Academy of Religion (AAR), not only to get more of a pulse on current and up-and-coming research, but to build some relationships with professors as well as with some graduate students who were doing kinds of work that I (thought I) wanted to do.

After a four-hour drive, my friend Chris and I met up with Chris's brother, Nick, who coincidentally was a doctoral student in one of the programs I was considering. Nick and his friends were at the conference early for another, smaller, scholarly meeting, so we joined their group, some grad students but mostly professors (two of whom had written books that I had on my bookshelf), at the bar. I was nervous, but I knew it was a big opportunity to connect with more senior scholars, so I took a deep breath and walked confidently into the bar.

I killed the meet and greet. And the AAR. I wore makeup and earrings and skirts, something I rarely did, let alone for four days straight, and spent much of the long weekend with these men. Sitting across and around from them at the bar, I professed my love for Dr. A's insightful research on the significance of Augustine's trinitarian thought for political theology, for Dr. L's creative and compelling analysis of the theological import of Kierkegaard's pseudonymous writings, for P's (he was too young to call professor, even though he was one) critique of normativity and reification of the status quo in much of natural theology. When they asked about me, I told them about a paper I'd written using Barth's examination of the enhypostasis of Christ alongside feminist analyses of gender. When they asked about the different feminist theorists I used and which I aligned most with, I talked about Butler's notion of performativity and the significance of deconstructing gender. They all nodded, intrigued. I took it as an opportunity to edge my way in even more.

"So, it's interesting," I mused. "Deconstruction aside [I think I rambled something about eschatology and sin and living between the "already-and-the-not-yet"], I noticed there are no other females here. Are there any girls coming to *any* of y'all's events [this scholarly meeting/group had some sessions sprinkled throughout official AAR activities]?"

"Do you want to come?" P asked.

"Sure," I said, trying to be as nonchalant as possible.

"Then yup, we'll have at least one woman there."

Woman. Not girl. I smiled to myself. My brief, beer-aided **performance as my then ideal, the girl who acts like a guy but doesn't look like one, my Walter Matthau-in-a-miniskirt** (Jürgen Moltmann in a pencil skirt?) **routine, had sold them.**

I continued the act throughout the conference, throughout my second master's, and a little bit into my first year as a doctoral student at Vanderbilt. But **this wasn't a performance I could sustain. No doubt** the professor who taught my first-semester doctoral seminar on the Doctrine of the Trinity: The Nicene Heritage—a professor I had met at that AAR just shy of two years ago—and most of my male colleagues (at least those who had seen me in prior contexts) were **confused when I began my work at Vanderbilt absent all chutzpah, nervous and anxious to please. I had presented, initially, as someone who pleased by not trying to: the cool girl.** My colleagues, at Vanderbilt and elsewhere, were mostly men, older than I was, and far more versed in systematic theology. **I liked them and envied their laid-back yet irascible attitudes, the ideal for** budding theologians. **Maybe they were naturally that way, or maybe I was so intimidated by my own inexperience that I only thought so.**

While I called myself a feminist, and took courses in women's and gender studies, I made sure to know just as much about systematics and to make sure that, whenever I talked feminism, I also talked Barth, or Bonhoeffer, or Aquinas, or Kierkegaard, because I thought that doing otherwise **would make me less desirable.** As a partnered queer woman, **this "desirability" was about my self-worth, not practical application. And yet, I was obsessed with the male gaze.** At the time, my interests were a bouquet of kitsch masculinity, with a tinge of feminism thrown in: the differences in the first and second edition of the *Römerbrief*, with a brief mention of Barth's little thing (whatever the hell it was) with Charlotte; waxing poetically about the significance of Augustine's phenomenology of the self in *De Trinitate*, while pointing out the very real misogynism he inherited from Aristotle. **I loved this male world of theology, and I loved the fact that I loved it.**

That year, I'd been reading a little about Judith Butler's theory of gender performativity, about how drag can reveal the socially constructed aspects of gender, and in a way, **subtly, subversively tweak it.** I thought that pursuing work in theological studies (**oh, it's such a boys' club**, everyone said, which thrilled me) was a little like that—dressing in drag.

But I was never as ironic as I tried to be. Really, I just wanted to be the girl who got into the boys' club.

At one point in the first month of my doctoral program, I was talking with a group of my colleagues in the graduate student lounge, and the conversation turned toward dissertation topics. They were discussing the merits of different projects, and were critiquing a recent graduate who had done work on feminism and ethnography.

Becoming a Feminist Theologian

They mused that her work wasn't "real theology," and that she was going to have a hard time finding a good job, and if she got one, it would be because she's a woman, not because of the merits of her scholarship. **I told that story to my friends later**, emphasizing the role of systematic theology in my work, foregrounding how I wanted to engage with Barth's notion of revelation and Bonhoeffer's Christology, minimizing how I wanted to explore those things in serious conversation with feminist theory. **Not even a month in, and I'd drunk the Kool-Aid.**

When I was in divinity school, not only were there few women in the program—the class after mine was over 70 percent male, and I knew more women who were spouses of students or worked as administrative assistants than female students—but there were especially very few women who were interested in *theology*: many were interested in ministry, some in nonprofit/social work type stuff, and a few in finding husbands. There were two in particular who stood out to me—that were interested in theology, but played the game very differently. **To me, they represented a choice of types: one woman** represented a sort of trophy wife, but a really cool and smart one. She was beautiful—model-like, really—but sweet, friendly, and laid-back. She dressed well, a combo of J. Crew and H&M, of put-together and not trying hard at all. She was confident but down-to-earth. Her husband was a doctor, and they were Baptist. And she had serious theological chops and could hold her own in conversations. We'll call her Kara. The second woman (I'll call her Caroline) was a queer tomboy **who was always casual and unruffled, sexy but never made up. She had a husky voice and a kind of relaxed swagger**, had tattoos, and was just a general badass. She even worked at a bar. She too could hold her own in theological conversations, but always would insert her radical queer eco-feminist concerns, regardless of the conversation. It awed me—she'd find ways to talk about ecology in Hegel or queer concerns in Kant, it was damned impressive—but it was so often perceived as a distraction from the real theological stuff, a derailing of genuine *theological* conversation. Kara **was in the boys' club**; Caroline **was not. I wanted to be a** Kara, even though, if I was honest with myself, I was far, far more of a Caroline.

The types themselves aren't important. The thing that's so discouraging to me now is that *I* **was doing this typing, both to**

other women and to myself, and that the right answer was the one the boys liked more.

I became simultaneously worried about being pretty enough and being *manly* enough—or perhaps about being manly enough and pretty enough. Some of my closest friends in div school were guys, and I remember my friend Steve and I having **one of those fungal arguments (it started small, but oh, how it bloomed)** about whether I was trying too hard to be one of the guys. That accusation has three stingers: that telling dirty jokes, playing beer pong, talking De Lubac, or pneumatology **equals "being a guy," that "trying too hard" is the gravest error, and that whether I was trying or not, I was definitely,** *definitely* **locked out.**

Spring of my first year, I was texting with a guy a few years ahead of me in my program. He knew I was struggling, and asked how it was going. "So I got a weird text from Mark, asking if you were a lesbian," he said. "Um, random," I remarked. "It's because you're so damn sexy, Brandy," he replied. "Every straight guy out there wants to hope it's not true!"

Sometimes, your radar is working even if you can't tell exactly what it's telling you. In that environment, the line between gross and professional, or gross and chummy, **could blur quickly, or else too slowly for you to realize, like a frog in hot water. In wanting** to be "in" as a girl in the boy's world of theology, **I'd jumped in the pot.** Of course I'd expected it to be a sexist environment, I just thought that wouldn't bother me. You know: "She's cool."

A few weeks later, that friend asked me to babysit his daughter while he and his wife went to a concert. I, being me, ever so eager to please, agreed. When he dropped his seven-month-old daughter off at my place, he made a passing comment, something along the lines of "brains, beauty, boldness, and babysitting, who could ask for more?" It was meant as a joke, perhaps as a compliment, or as an odd way of saying thanks, but it struck me. "**Yep**," I laughed, "I've got it all," I joked, **too embarrassed to** say anything else.

It was such a small moment, but it was *the* **moment. No, I didn't like** his comment, **but I was more upset about my own** response, or rather, lack thereof. Despite trying so hard to be one of "them" I had failed. I wasn't enough of a Kara or enough of a Caroline. **I was not in the boys' club.** It wasn't until a bit later that I finally got that Kara was not "a Kara" and Caroline was not "a Caroline," **and that maybe**

my colleagues' **sexist typing of me wasn't any worse than my own. I also realized then that Kara wasn't in the boys' club like I had thought she was. And that's the moment I remember as the beginning** not of my own feminism—as I said, I identified as a feminist throughout all of this—but as a feminist theologian (in training). It was then that I stopped trying to fit into the theological "mainstream"—what I perceived as the theological mainstream!—and just decided to do my own thing and care about what I cared about, regardless of what "box" it put me in, or what boxes it precluded me from. This realization, of course, **took a while to jell.** In fact, I think it is still jelling, still forming.

This isn't to lump together all the men in theology, or to suggest that I was trampled in some hog-call of cigar-smoking pigs in velvet jackets. What I learned in divinity school and especially in my first year of my doctoral program **is that I had so deeply internalized sexism that I didn't see it even when it was looking right at me from all directions: that sometimes, those eyes were the only eyes that I'd see.**

To want to break into the boys' club *because* it is a boys' club, you must believe that it's worth breaking into. Like the fantasy of taming a wild animal, having the meanest dog on the block, or dating men who don't like women very much, the promise of earned entrance to a boys' club is that you will feel chosen, *exceptional*: you are not like the others. You have transcended your gender. And you have done this not because you think your gender shouldn't matter as much as it does, but because you think the boys' club must be better than any of the clubs that will have you.

That one took—is still taking?—**a long time to unlearn.**

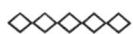

Unwomanly Me?
Further Reflections on Doing Gender in the Theological Academy

After posting my theological spin on Scherm's essay, I received a good number of comments, and even more emails, from both women and men, commiserating about this desire to be a part of the boys' club. One theme that emerged from follow-up conversations was the difficulty of disentangling the source of one's desires.[9] While on the one hand, there was internalized sexism at play (among other factors), there was also genuine interest in things that were traditionally seen as masculine. And while the desire to *conform* to be a part of the boys' club was real, there was also the desire to do the things that happened to be under the purview of the boys' club. Was my interest in some obscure systematic theologians genuine, or was it about my effort to show how knowledgeable and passionate I was about systematics? What about my interest in arguing in general, or my interest in West Coast IPAs? Was that "authentic," was it an effort to fit in, or was it both? It has often seemed that being a woman in theology meant being stuck between a rock and a hard place—a reality that, as Serene Jones put it, is true in terms of how you understand and interpret "women's experience," but also seems true in, well, the experience itself.[10]

Women in Theology has itself reflected some of this reality. In her post "On Not Reading Barth," Janice McRandal reflected on one small way she sought to not merely avoid but to resist the tokenism that comes with being the sole woman in academic theological environments—by, as the title suggests, not reading Barth.[11] Soon after McRandal's post, Kaitlyn Dugan, the then curator (now director) of the Center for Barth Studies at Princeton Theological Seminary, wrote a response post on her own blog, entitled "On Reading Barth."[12] Whereas for McRandal, *not* reading Barth means resisting "the production and control of 'serious scholarship,'" *reading* Barth—critically engaging and appropriating Barth, putting him "in profound and rigorous bilateral dialogue [with] other critical theologians in order to create something new"—accomplished those same aims. Whereas McRandal reflected on feeling isolated and tokenized in theological studies given her theological priorities that meant not reading Barth, Dugan, who affirmed and supported McRandal's approach, reflected on feeling alienated as a female theologian who did read Barth. McRandal and Dugan's respective experiences, like my own, point to how gender norms, desire, and power converge through, and are reflected in, these kinds of double binds. Moreover, the responses to their respective posts are also telling and speak further to the isolation women face in theology. Whereas McRandal's post engendered a significant amount of pushback and criticism, those critics did not in turn celebrate Dugan's post.[13] McRandal and Dugan's respective experiences highlight the rock and hard place that female theologians are so often stuck between.

More significantly, in telling the truth about their experiences as women in the theological academy, McRandal and Dugan draw implicitly on the feminist theological tradition—a tradition especially emphasized and uplifted by womanist and mujerista theologians—of turning to lived experience as a site and source of theological truth and subsequent potential sociopolitical change.[14] Moreover, in doing so, they begin to point to, and create space for, a way forward beyond representational politics. The "insistence upon the coherence and unity of the category of women has effectively refused the multiplicity of cultural, social, and political intersections in which the concrete array of 'women' are constructed," Butler writes in their groundbreaking book *Gender Trouble*.[15] A site by and for women in theology can, and perhaps does, run the risk of excluding those who are even more marginalized and oppressed for their gender identity and expression.[16] Yet the diversity of experiences and voices of female theologians on sites like, and beyond, *Women in Theology*, reflect no such insistence, and point to the ways in which power, via both desire and alienation, cuts in multiple directions across and through lines of gender, sexuality, class, race, and so on—the ways in which power in fact "operate[s] in the production of that very binary frame for thinking about gender."

A question Butler, building on Foucault, later asks—"Who can I be, given the regime of truth that determines ontology for me?"—is a question that undergirds posts like McRandal's, Dugan's, and my own.[17] In asking and making space for those questions, feminist theologians, and sites like *Women in Theology*, also begin to open up space for new possibilities for how we understand and do gender in and beyond the theological academy.

NOTES

1. For feminist, womanist, and mujerista theological scholarship on this front, see especially Mary McClintock Fulkerson, *Changing the Subject: Women's Discourses and Feminist Theology* (Minneapolis: Augsburg Fortress, 1994); Katie G. Cannon, *Katie's*

Cannon: Womanism and the Soul of the Black Community (New York: Continuum, 1998); Stacy Floyd-Thomas, *Mining the Motherlode: Methods in Womanist Ethics* (Cleveland: Pilgrim Press, 2006); Ada María Isasi-Díaz, *En La Lucha/In the Struggle: Elaborating a Mujerista Theology* (Minneapolis: Fortress Press, 2004 [1994]); Linda Hogan, *From Women's Experience to Feminist Theology* (New York: Bloomsbury Academic, 1995). For research on women's experiences in academia, see the research compiled by Anna Goeddeke and Louisa Söllner on the website *Women in Academia*, https://sites.google.com/view/womeninacademia/home.

2. See *An und für sich*, https://itself.blog/ (started by Adam Kotsko and Anthony Paul Smith); *Faith and Theology*, https://www.faith-theology.com/ (started by Ben Myers); and *Die Evangelischen Theologen*, https://derevth.blogspot.com/ (started by Travis McMaken).

3. I do want to note that while *An un für sich* was a particularly intense space with a rather combative ethos that could easily be read as having a masculine energy (especially given that the contributors and commenters were predominately male), it was also one of the first blog sites to engage the topic of gender and the theoblogosphere and to give me space to express my own voice around said topics. See especially Anthony Paul Smith, "On the Culture of Fear in Theology: More on Gender and Theology," *An und für sich*, December 4, 2012, https://itself.blog/2012/12/04/on-the-culture-of-fear-in-theology-more-on-gender-and-theology/.

4. See Julia, "Beginning: Holding the Horn," *WIT: Women in Theology*, October 9, 2010, https://womenintheology.org/ 2010/10/09/beginning/.

5. Before I was a part of *Women in Theology*, I ended up blogging about the gift of the pink penis-shaped water gun and my experience as a woman in theology (on *An und für sich* where, as noted previously, I had the opportunity to talk about gender in this way for the first time). See Brandy Daniels, "Gender and Theology (and the Theological Academy): A Response to Tony Baker's 'Gender and the Studio'—Part One," *An und für sich*, November 26, 2012, https://itself.blog/2012/11/26/gender-and-theology-and-the-theological-academy-a-response-to-tony-bakers-gender-and-the-studio-part-one/.

6. Kampen, "Feminism, Trans Visibility, and Gender Politics in Theology," *An und für sich*, March 31, 2016, https://itself.blog/2016/03/31/feminism-trans-visibility-and-gender-politics-in-theology/.

7. Rebecca Scherm, "Manly Me," *The Hairpin*, July 18, 2013, https://www.thehairpin.com/2013/07/manly-me/.

8. Brandy Daniels, "Manly Me (Theology Edition)," *WIT: Women in Theology*, August 23, 2013, https://womenintheology.org/2013/08/23/manly-me-theology-edition/. Passages in bold are from Scherm's work and are used with permission.

9. I reflected on this in a subsequent blog post—see Brandy Daniels, "Un-womanly Me? (A Post about, and Full of, Paradoxes)," *WIT: Women in Theology*, September 9, 2013, https://womenintheology.org/2013/09/09/un-womanly-me-a-post-about-and-full-of-paradoxes/.

10. See Serene Jones, "Women's Experience between a Rock and a Hard Place," in *Horizons in Feminist Theology: Identity, Tradition, and Norms*, ed. Rebecca S. Chopp and Sheila Greeve Davaney (Minneapolis: Fortress Press, 1997), 33–53.

11. Janice McRandal, "On Not Reading Barth: My Measly Resistance," *WIT: Women in Theology*, September 1, 2013, https://womenintheology.org/2013/09/01/on-not-reading-barth-my-measly-resistance/. See her revised version of this post in the next chapter.

12. Kait Dugan, "On Reading Barth: Another Form of Feminist Resistance," *Kyrie Eleison*, September 2, 2013, https://kaitdugan.blogspot.com/2013/09/on-reading-barth-another-form-of.html.

13. However, when a male theologian wrote a follow-up post affirming McRandal's post, his post received a slew of appreciative responses for his honesty and thoughtfulness. See Peter Kline, "On Not Reading Karl Barth Anymore: A White Male's Perspective," *Faith and Theology*, September 5, 2013, https://www.faith-theology.com/2013/09/on-not-reading-karl-barth-anymore-white.html.

14. See n. 1 above.

15. Judith Butler, *Gender Trouble: Feminism and the Subversion of Identity* (New York: Routledge, 1999), xxvii.

16. See Kampen, "Feminism, Trans Visibility, and Gender Politics in Theology."

17. Judith Butler, *Giving an Account of Oneself* (New York: Fordham University Press, 2005), 25.

3

STILL NOT READING BARTH

Janice McRandal

On September 1, 2013, I posted my second-ever blog post, knowing very well that I was about to deeply upset a determined and loud element of the Christian theological community. It was a blog post that came nine days after I had submitted my doctoral thesis for examination. The timing was not insignificant—I'd finally fulfilled my requirements as a research student in systematic theology and could now offer a candid, less fearful, evaluation of the theological community I had unwittingly joined. It was a blogsphere event that marked me in ways I am still mapping and tracing today. What follows comes in two parts: the original post of 2013 and a new post, if you like, or a reception history that is at once coolly objective and deeply personal. A further foray into the subculture's furor over a nobody Australian woman who didn't want to read the Swiss theologian, Karl Barth. And as the chapter title makes clear, I am still here, still not reading Barth.

On Not Reading Barth: My Measly Resistance

But I was never as ironic as I tried to be.
 Really, I just wanted to be the girl who got into the boys' club.[1]

Still Not Reading Barth

I am sure I am not the only woman in theology who resonated deeply with Brandy's most recent post.[2] That Brandy raised the obvious similarities—of discerning the depths of sexism and patriarchy—of women across various fields highlighted the way "excellence" or even "appropriate development" in professional environments is entangled by the patriarchal paradigm, a patriarchy that goes all the way down. As I have previously shared, all my postgraduate study has occurred in an environment where I have been the sole woman studying systematic theology. I have enjoyed genuine friendship with all the men in my program, and to be honest, in the latter stages of thesis writing these men provided solidarity that I was quite literally desperate for. However, it has always been hard for me to express something of my experience as (what often felt like) the "token women," and as a feminist trying to find a path in the cultural landscape of systematic theology. It has been even harder for me—and has taken years to find a way—to critique the field of systematic theology among those whose friendship I have hoped for and needed, especially when that critique involves an area of research they are involved in. For that reason, I have often kept quiet about my concerns regarding the culture of scholarship in systematic theology (and especially the subcultures that I have found myself "lucky" enough to engage with). It has been far easier to offer substantive feedback regarding a theological argument than to confront the broader institution. Often this has meant engaging in private, even secretive, strategies of resistance.

Four and a half years ago I made the decision to not read Karl Barth. It was a personal and private commitment that I felt I could not really share with anyone. The reasoning seemed (and still does at some level) naïve and rather embarrassing, and I was sure that the men around me would not understand. Certainly my "not reading Barth as a matter of principle" has been a strategy built upon various personal experiences that are obviously far from universal. And to be clear, this strategy has little to do with my taste or distaste for Barth's scholarship—to which I felt deeply drawn in all my undergraduate studies. Nor do I simply ignore how large his figure looms, or the enormous influence of dialectical theology per se. Rather, my commitment to not reading Barth arose because of my concerns regarding the institution of Barthian scholarship and my understanding of identity for theologians on the margins. By not reading Barth I was, and have been, engaging in what I believe is a form of resistance, a small gesture I could manage as I tried to find a voice and place beyond tokenism. There are several ways in which I have understood this as resistance.

First, this has been a means to resist the production and control of "serious scholarship." It is no secret that systematic theologians have consistently critiqued contextual theologies for lacking rigor. I learned early in postgraduate studies that if I were to be a feminist that distanced herself from contextual theology, my male counterparts would (instantly) take me more seriously. In the canon of Protestant scholarship, the rigors of Barth studies and Hegelian philosophy serve as a green card into the world of serious scholarship. I clearly remember thinking that I too could dive into the *Dogmatics*[3] and carve out an identity as the "woman Barth scholar" (keep in mind that the theological community in Australia is rather small) who is a "serious theologian." And yet my identity as a young woman feminist demanded that I critique these claims of "serious scholarship." This has been a difficult journey, especially as I have found myself drawn to women scholars who have become the litmus test for serious feminist scholarship (Sarah Coakley and Kathryn Tanner, for example). And of course, to be published and employed one must prove themselves to be rigorous in their approach. Still, the further I became engaged in circles of systematic theology, it was Barth who was proven the definitive voice in the major issues of Protestant scholarship. It was clear time and time again that many around me felt a failure to consult Barth in numerous areas of doctrinal debate was a failure to engage in serious scholarship. I felt (and still feel) that it was not only legitimate to, but also that I had to, resist this.

Second, by not reading Barth I am attempting to resist "confessional identity." By this I am referring to the way in which "Barth" is invoked as the magic word for Protestant "orthodoxy." I am both tired and bored of the liberal/conservative melodramatic critique of modernity in which Barthian orthodoxy gets to play the tall, dark, and handsome hero in every performance (I have deployed this all-too-easy tactic myself). Not only has this typology become an almost crude cliché, but the claims to orthodoxy also continue to function as a silencer of the radical, and nearly always a silencer of those speaking from the margins. Consequently, systematic theology continually evades the challenges raised by those outside the guild and status quo is maintained through the hypercontrol of orthodoxy. Feminists have been silenced and ignored by these tactics for decades. Of course, there are feminist Barthians, and there are minoritized scholars working with various forms of Barthian theology. However, nearly every time I have read Barthian scholarship and glanced over the footnotes I have been struck by how (obviously) this culture of systematic theology supports white men talking about what other white men have said. Even those I know to support feminism in general largely fail to consult nonwhite men in their own scholarship (and yet strangely become defensive when questioned about this). It is as if "orthodoxy" really has nothing to do with the concerns of nonwhite men and those in the know don't care. Yes, one could argue "all the more reason to get involved," but I have felt it even better to simply resist furthering the conversation.

Third—and perhaps this is the best way to make the first two points—by resisting Barthian scholarship I have hoped to resist "institutional powers." From my perspective, Barthian scholarship seems a power unto itself. It seems an American Protestant power unto itself. When I attend conferences in America it is the Barthians who stand out, who have the large crowds, who have the "big names." What stands out is in fact the white men's club. It is like watching the powerful movement of patriarchy striding confidently on its long, able legs while wearing leather-patched tweed jackets. You often hear the lament of the "poor white scholar": "It is so hard not to be a queer, Black, disabled, liberal biblicist," we are told. It is the trump card of all institutional powers: "What momentum? There is no power here, we are now the minority!" Last year while attending the American Academy of Religion annual meeting I slipped off to a session at the Society of Biblical Literature to hear some "legends" of minoritized biblical scholarship. There were fourteen people in the room, including the five panelists. Don't believe the hype; the man is still the man, and the institution holds all the cards. In systematic theology American Barthianism epitomizes this.

So I think for now I will go on not reading Barth. It is a measly form of resistance. I know that. But it seems that for those on the margins to resist the lure of the center, there at least needs to be some recognition of how any theological culture defines the center and locates the power associated with serious scholarship and the enormity of claims pressed upon "orthodoxy." I don't expect to have too much influence, and in all my hypocrisy I know I am not a great revolutionary. But where I have the energy to resist I will, and I might not keep it a secret next time.

"Not Reading Barth Is a Bit Like Book Burning"

"Joe" commented on the *Women in Theology* blog post within twenty-four hours and his assessment of my post was clear: "I detest this sort of childish, adolescent, immature, negative, resentful, and profoundly stupid attitude to the greatest theologian of the 20th century."[4] In those first hours, I thought Joe's comment that "not reading Barth is a bit like book burning" was in equal measures extreme and comical, but as the days unfolded Joe's remark proved incisive. There were over two dozen responses published in the weeks that followed and almost all read my piece as a call to censorship.[5] From responses titled "On Not Hating Barth,"[6] to accusations of "academic fundamentalism,"[7] response after response projected a deep and unwavering concern for both my alleged censorship project and the absolute and urgent need for people everywhere to be reading Karl Barth! Even from the self-proclaimed "sympathetic" side, David Congdon insisted that while the "decision to not read Barth is utterly irrelevant and inconsequential" to any of my specific concerns, it's more likely "counterproductive," offering a predictable ethical imperative to go on reading Barth as "the surest way to right the wrongs of the past and ensure that Barth's theology does not scar the lives of others."[8] The fever pitch of these readings is perhaps no more obvious than in the four separate posts by the—at the time enormously influential—biblio-blogger, James E. (Jim) West.[9] West has unsurprisingly featured in numerous theology blog/Twitter controversies, some of which he has recorded on his own Wikipedia page. Regarding my blog post, first he said that the public conversations taking place about the piece, in which some people were stating they had also chosen to not read Barth, were "boasting of ignorance," arguing "what a witless world we occupy when people pretending to be academics are thrilled to be uninformed and even more thrilled to tell others how uninformed they are."[10] It is telling that in the comment section, West has the original article pointed out to him and he shows zero interest in acknowledging the conversation starter or the concerns raised in the post. However, in his post on September 9 he reposted a direct response to the original post, making plain his awareness and complete indifference to the issues raised in my post and repeating his censorship claims. He then reduced conversation participants (reposting another response to *me*) to "angry anti-Barthians," and reiterated the censorship claims, writing of the "absurd campaign to dissuade thinkers from reading [Barth]." Rounding off his commentary on the public conversation with a typically emotional and ludicrous interpretation: "It's like debating whether we should be smart or stupid. Apparently, stupidity and ignorance has [*sic*] champions. And defenders." Repeating his warnings against (my) censorship project he called his readers to "ignore Barth's enemies."[11]

What are we—I—to make of these extreme reactions? Rereading my own words all these years later, I've been struck by the transparent attempts I made in the original post to situate my concerns, writing of a "strategy built upon various personal experiences that are obviously far from universal." And, "Of course, there are feminist Barthians, and there are minoritized scholars working with various forms of Barthian theology." The blog title itself acknowledged the *measly* form of resistance I was engaging in, so it is hard to receive these interpretations outside of the long history of ignoring women's substantive critiques for the holy cause of defending great men and the great men traditions we hold dear. It's telling that the only two published responses that engaged and thought with my critiques without ridiculous claims of censorship or demanding that I keep reading Barth came from a sole women's voice—Kait Dugan, who could speak to experience of being the sole women *inside* the world of Barth studies—and a former Princeton Barthian, Peter Kline, who could witness to the abusive subculture and the power it held.[12] As the weeks, months, and even years have passed, I have continued to receive private messages and emails, imploring me that I simply must read Karl Barth, and not a single follow up to my critique of the theological industry or vulnerable sharing of life as a feminist theologian in spaces of isolation. One could almost imagine these conditions are not real.

And yet predictably, in the years since publishing "On Not Reading Barth," the Barth industry has only grown. For example, the Barth Studies stream at Aberdeen University has increased the number of Barth specialist faculty members and proudly publishes an almost exclusively male list of recent graduates and publications.[13] In 2015, the Australian and New Zealand Association of Theological Schools introduced the first and still only research group named after a sole theological figure, the Karl Barth group. And in 2018, the already richly resourced Center for Barth Studies at Princeton Seminary was awarded a National Endowment for the Humanities (NEH) translation grant of $300,000 with a further grant awarded in 2021.[14] The Center for Barth Studies has since initiated a strategic philanthropy project and you can now donate $10,000 to furthering the Barth industry with the click of a button.[15] To those inside these richly resourced theological communities, it is hard to convey the contrast of a feminist theologian in Australia, which was of course the experience I was at pains to share. To this day, I am still the only feminist theologian to have been the lecturer in systematic theology in an Australian theological college. Only one college in all of Australia runs a feminist theology class, proving that feminist theology subjects are deemed far too controversial among the conservative Australian colleges.[16] And while a center for feminist theological studies was established in 2015, it has been denied funding time and time again, scrounging around for a thousand dollars here and there while the institutions around it insist that attending to "gender injustice" is key strategic matter.[17] David Congdon was irrefutably right, my "decision to not read Barth [was] utterly irrelevant and inconsequential." However, if any of Barth's esteemed defenders were paying much attention, they would have understood that this was in part, *precisely my point.*

My measly resistance was to develop a strategy to survive and navigate this world. A strategy for me in my context. I had no idea then how deep was the affect of the great men of academia. Nor did I truly appreciate the force of history that was being defended in the responses to my post. It was not only that Barth belonged to a canon of "serious scholarship" one must study in the hope of any credibility, but it was also the function of these figures as a singularity, a singular project, a singular strategy, or bust. Hence, I could *only* be read as a book-burning censor. Approaching a decade later, it is clear to me now how those of us trained in the humanities are encouraged, resourced, pushed, to specialize in the thoughts and tradition of a single thinker, a Man. Entire communities of disciples form and gather around the subject/object of our devotion, leading to named-after-the-Man journals and conferences and chaired positions and, more recently, merchandise. Feminist theology, however, has not yet generated this same myopic approach to academia, an approach that can be mapped according to the logic of the one. I take this to be a very good sign. And I continue to ignore the repeated demands to engage these great thinkers centered within the imperium of esteemed scholarship.

In 2017, philosopher Sara Ahmed published *Living a Feminist Life*.[18] It was a text and strategy that gave (me) more words to my measly resistance and to the experience I had described of being a feminist engaging doctoral studies in the humanities. As she notes in the opening of her book, "When I was doing my PhD, I was told I had to give my love to this or that male theorist, to follow him, not necessarily as an explicit command but through an apparently gentle but increasingly insistent questioning: Are you a Derridean; no, so are you a Lacanian, no, oh, okay, so are you a Deleuzian; no, then what?"[19] As Ahmed recalls, she was unwilling, like I had been, to agree with this demand. However, in *Living a Feminist Life*, she takes her refusal to a new level, initiating a strict citation policy. She writes,

> In this book I adopt a strict citation policy: I do not cite any white men. By white men I am referring to an institution....Instead, I cite those who have contributed to the intellectual genealogy of feminism and antiracism, including work that has been too quickly (in my view) cast aside or left behind, work that lays out other paths, paths we can call desire lines, created by not following the official paths laid out by disciplines.[20]

For Ahmed, this entails a citation policy that centers the memory of feminists of color as a strategic way of constructing new dwellings of feminist discourses, and crucially, new ways of being in the world—of living a feminist life. This publication helped me to further articulate the kind of personal practices I had been developing and to understand the way my "On Not Reading Barth" had largely been received. In a chapter on diversity work within intuitional systems, Ahmed states it bluntly: "A system is working when an attempt to transform that system is blocked."[21]

However, it is clear to me that my blog post was never an attempt to transform the industry of Barth studies. Not even close. Rather, it was a deeply personal proclamation, one that has carried me through into my professional academic life beyond doctoral studies. This is a strategy, and an outside, outlier, approach to the force of Western history that is definitely not the only strategy available to any one of us. To take it up is not to lay down a law. It is, as Ahmed makes clear, *to choose a way of life*. And without a skerrick of doubt or hesitation, I stand by my choice.

NOTES

1. Janice McRandal, "On Not Reading Barth: My Measly Resistance," *WIT: Women in Theology*, September 1, 2013, https://womenintheology.org/2013/09/01/on-not-reading-barth-my-measly-resistance/. This post references other pieces published by *Women in Theology* that are not included in this current collection. I have chosen to include my post exactly as it was published as a historical record that can be exegeted in the current day.

2. Brandy Daniels has included her original post as part of her chapter in this volume, "Becoming a Feminist Theologian: On Doing Gender in the Theological Academy."

3. For those not familiar with Karl Barth, his major systematic work is a twelve-volume set called *Church Dogmatics*. Those in Barth studies refer to it as "the *Dogmatics*."

4. "Joe," commenter on the original blog post.

5. Many of these are no longer available online. Some belong to blog accounts now made private and some to defunct blogs no longer in existence. Pingbacks on the original *Women in Theology* post along with those posted on Facebook confirm a total of twenty-six published responses in the first two weeks.

6. "On Hating Karl Barth," *Neighborly Theology*, September 9, 2013. No longer available online.

7. Joel Watts, "On Not Reading Barth—Or, Academic Fundamentalism," *Unsettled Christianity*, September 10, 2013. No longer available online.

8. David Congdon, "On Still Reading Barth: Some Sympathetic Reflections," *The Fire and the Rose*, September 10, 2013. https://fireandrose.blogspot.com/2013/09/on-still-reading-barth-some-sympathetic.html.

9. West continues to blog daily at *Zwinglius Redivivus*, zwingliusredivivus.wordpress.com.

10. Jim West, "Proud of Ignorance," *Zwinglius Redivivus*, September 2, 2013, https://zwingliusredivivus.wordpress.com/2013/09/02/proud-of-ignorance/.

11. Jim West, "Barth with All His Faults Should Still Be Read," *Zwinglius Redivivus*, September 9, 2013, https://zwingliusredivivus.wordpress.com/2013/09/09/barth-with-all-his-faults-should-still-be-read/ and Jim West, "You're Right, Chris, the 'Debate' about Reading Barth or Not Is Weird," *Zwinglius Redivivus*, September 10, 2013, https://zwingliusredivivus.wordpress.com/2013/09/10/youre-right-chris-the-debate-about-reading-barth-or-not-is-weird/.

12. Kait Dugan, "On Reading Barth: Another Form of Feminist Resistance (a Response to Janice Rees)," *Kyrie Eleison*, September 2, 2013, http://kaitdugan.blogspot.com/2013/09/on-reading-barth-another-form-of.html and Peter Kline, "On Not Reading Karl Barth Anymore: A White Male's Perspective," *Faith and Theology*, September 5, 2013, https://www.faith-theology.com/2013/09/on-not-reading-karl-barth-anymore-white.html.

13. Barth Studies page, Aberdeen University, https://www.abdn.ac.uk/sdhp/divinity-religious-studies/barth-studies-1179.php#panel1192.

14. "Princeton Seminary Receives NEH Grant to Translate Renowned Theologian's Works into English," Princeton Theological Seminary, August 9, 2018, https://www.ptsem.edu/news/center-for-barth-studies-neh-grant.

15. Center for Barth Studies Giving page, Princeton Theological Seminary, https://inside.ptsem.edu/open/giving/giveBarth.aspx.

16. The only full feminist theology units available to formally study in Australia are offered through Pilgrim Theological College, https://divinity.edu.au/entity/fem/study/.

17. Australian Collaborators in Feminist Theologies, https://divinity.edu.au/entity/fem/.

18. Sara Ahmed, *Living a Feminist Life* (Durham, NC: Duke University Press, 2017).

19. Ahmed, *Living a Feminist Life*, 15.

20. Ahmed, *Living a Feminist Life*, 15.

21. Ahmed, *Living a Feminist Life*, 97.

4

THÉOLOGIENNE, THÉOLOGIEN, THEOLOGIAN?

Feminist Historical Theology from Angélique Arnauld to Mary Daly

Elissa Cutter

As an academic theologian and blogger who works on an allegedly heretical group of nuns from seventeenth-century France, I have thought about the power of naming and the role of language in shaping our understanding of reality both historically and today.[1] Specifically, each time I read Mary Daly's *Beyond God the Father*, I continue to think about her arguments concerning naming and language in relation to the polemics against the nuns that are my current research focus, namely the Port-Royal nuns.[2] Daly's text makes a critique of our use of language because "the entire conceptual systems of theology and ethics, developed under the conditions of patriarchy, have been the products of males and tend to serve the interests of sexist society."[3] In this, she called for an entire rethinking of the way we speak about the world. Now, the reason the Port-Royal nuns are so interesting to me in relation to this is because the debate

Théologienne, Théologien, Theologian?

around them raised questions about their ability to read and produce theology—both whether one could understand them as doing theology and as proposing a new way of doing theology, one that was separate from the universities of the time. In what follows, I explore the way feminist historical theology offers us a methodological resource for recovering women's voices as theologians—like those of the Port-Royal nuns—and why this task remains important today.

In part my interest in the Port-Royal nuns comes precisely from my perspective as a feminist historical theologian. This means that as a historical theologian, I study the ideas expressed in history and look at them in context to evaluate and argue for what ideas we should maintain today and which ones might be no longer useful (if they ever were). In this, I take inspiration from the definition of historical theology proposed by Patrick Carey, who argued,

> Historical theology tries to shed light on the ideas and the tradition that transcend the multiple historical incarnations, and on the ideas and systems of theological thinking that have either been captured by the times in which they emerged or were so conditioned by the languages and conceptions of their day that they have outlived their usefulness and are alien to the contemporary world for which historical theologians write.[4]

As a *feminist* theologian, a lens that I use to evaluate ideas is whether they are liberative or oppressive to women—namely, if they support the idea that both men and women "have the same dignity as creatures made in [God's] image and likeness."[5] We need to remember in looking at past ideas that there is, rooted in human dignity, a "radical equality" among men and women—of "all people, regardless of their race, nation, sex, origin, culture, or class."[6] The social teaching of the Catholic Church asks us to ensure "conditions of equal opportunity for men and women" and that "the feminine genius" be present "in all expressions in the life of society," so the work that I do in studying the history of theological teaching is to evaluate what ideas can help us today to ensure such conditions.[7] Of course, the church emphasizes not only the equality but the difference between men and women.[8] But maintaining such an idea of difference does not prevent us from evaluating both whether theological ideas create the equal opportunity that the church calls us to work for and whether these ideas support women's full dignity as made in the image of God. In fact, the Catholic teaching on the difference and complementarity between men and women further supports creating such conditions of equal opportunity, especially in listening to the voices and experiences of women. That is, because "man and woman complete each other mutually, not only from a physical and psychological point of view, but also ontologically," the church should also value the perspectives and ideas of women and see women's experience as contributing to our full understanding of what it means to be human.[9] Thus, following the examples of other feminist theologians, my overall methodological approach applies this lens to the writings by and about women in the history of Christianity to recover their voices and determine what we can learn from them today.[10]

To illustrate this approach, we can return to the example of the Port-Royal nuns. The convent of Port-Royal was a Cistercian convent located in the valley of Chevreuse, southwest of Paris. In 1602, Jacqueline Arnauld became abbess there at the age of eleven, taking the name of Angélique.[11] She had obtained this position because of the connections her grandfather had with the Cistercian order and the king of France, and by her family lying about her age. At the time she took possession of the convent, the nuns had let the rules of religious life lapse, including those governing the sharing of property and keeping the cloister. In 1609, following the inspiration she received from a visiting preacher's sermon on the incarnation and Christ's humility in becoming human, Mother Angélique began to reform the convent according to the guidelines of the Council of Trent and the Cistercian tradition, especially in following the *Rule of Saint Benedict* more strictly.[12] These reforms included putting all property in common, simplifying the habits of the nuns, eliminating meat from their diets, and implementing the cloister. The drama of this reform of the cloister occurred when her family came to see her at the convent and she refused them entrance, an event that is now known as the "day of the grille."

Because of her reform, Angélique encountered many of the key actors in the Catholic reform of seventeenth-century France, including Francis de Sales and Jeanne de Chantal. Eventually, however, she associated the convent with Jean Duvergier de Hauranne, known primarily by his title as the abbot of Saint-Cyran. Saint-Cyran was a

Théologienne, Théologien, Theologian?

prominent figure in reform movements in this period. Significantly, he had studied and then remained friends with Cornelius Jansen, for whom the movement known as Jansenism was named. Scholars characterize this movement by an Augustinian understanding of grace and human freedom, a rigorist interpretation of sacramental practices—especially for confession—and an extreme hatred of the Jesuits.[13] It is most properly identified as such following the posthumous publication of Jansen's *Augustinus* in 1640. There remains a difficulty in using these characteristics to identify someone as heretical or not in this period of history, however, because these three characteristics were common in France at this time. The convent of Port-Royal and its associates became the core of this allegedly heretical movement.

The debate over Jansenism and Port-Royal ended up focusing on the question of the nuns' knowledge of theology, specifically whether they understood the content of the *Augustinus* and, thus, had the ability to condemn Cornelius Jansen's work. This debate is part of why I see the nuns as so significant to recover as theological voices from the early modern era. The archbishop of Paris asked the nuns to sign a formulary that said that they agreed with the condemnation of five propositions about grace *and* that these five condemned propositions appeared in Jansen's *Augustinus*. The nuns' defenders argued in part that the nuns did not have the ability to judge whether the propositions appeared in the text because they did not concern themselves with questions of theology and, not knowing Latin, had not read the text itself. Antoine Arnauld asked in 1655, "What pretext can they have for spreading their persecution against virtuous nuns, who understand nothing in all these matters of theology, who have never read the least line about all these contested questions, and who make a particular vow to avoid all kinds of contention, in order to occupy themselves solely with the faithful observation of the Gospel and of their Rule?"[14] His claim here is that the nuns did not have any knowledge of theology—not only had they not read the text of the *Augustinus* or other texts discussing the question of grace and human freedom ("never read the least line about all these contested questions"), but they cared only to follow the practices of their order.

In contrast, the opponents of the nuns used the accusation of the nuns as *théologiennes* to argue that they were part of the theological controversy and that their theological knowledge meant that they were messing with things that should remain beyond their competence as women.[15] These anti-Jansenists texts illustrate for us the negative views of the relationship between women and theology throughout the history of the Catholic Church, a legacy that unfortunately—and in spite of the social teaching of the church about the equality of men and women—remains today. For example, we see this in the 1660 *Relation du pays de Jansenie*, an anti-Jansenist text written in the form of a travel diary by Louis Fontaines. "Louis Fontaines" was the pseudonym for Zacharie de Lisieux, a Capuchin who was known for his satirical works against the Jansenists. In this text, he mocked the "Janseniens" for teaching women and argued that they "are so zealous to their way, for the propagation of their faith, that they not only delegate men to establish it where it has not yet been received, but even female missionaries who bravely explain their theology. That is to say, that in Jansenie there are professors of both sexes, and that the doctrine there had fallen into the hands of women [*en quenoüille*]."[16] The term used here, *en quenoüille*, had become figuratively used in genealogy to refer to following the feminine line of the family and, by extension "to a woman who wants to meddle in the affairs of the husband, things that she does not understand."[17] Thus, this text argued that the women among the "Janseniens" meddled with theology, something beyond their understanding as women.

Opponents of Jansenism often attacked the Port-Royal nuns in these texts to discredit male figures associated with them. For example, Jean de Brisacier wrote a text against the Irish priest John Callaghan who had studied in France and had ties to the convent of Port-Royal. In the foreword to his text, Brisacier connected Callaghan to Port-Royal, which Brisacier described as "conforming to [Callaghan's] erroneous opinions" and as the place that "began this gruesome revolt which has gone on for so long against the Holy See."[18] Brisacier's text followed in a long tradition of using the trope of the heretical women as a way to discredit male heretics.[19] For example, Brisacier argued that the heretics "borrow the mouth and the ministry of women in order to spread their poison." He then provides a litany of heretics with their female associates, one that can be found verbatim in the letters of Jerome.[20] Brisacier wrote,

> Simon Magnus was made nothing without his Helena, most gruesome in the world and more renowned than that

Théologienne, Théologien, Theologian?

of Troy, Apelles without his Philumena, Donatus without his Lucilla, Montanus without his two female apostles Priscilla and Maximilla, and all the other heretics might have never made great progress in their gospel of error without the help of women. And always and everywhere that there is reborn some old Adam in order to lose the world again, he would not come to the end without his Eve.

Thus, Brisacier borrowed the litany of heretics found in Jerome's writings to make his ultimate point of contrast between heretical and orthodox movements, namely that the heretics allow women to preach and teach, while "a Catholic preacher imposes silence on women with Saint Paul."[21] Given that this trope of the heretical woman began in the early church and survived for so much of the church's history, I am not surprised that women today still have to struggle to have our equality recognized—as the *Compendium* calls for—and our voices heard.

These examples often made general references to the nuns of Port-Royal without naming the individual nuns directly, but the *Mémoire* written by Sébastien Zamet in 1638 against Saint-Cyran identified his influence as leading the nuns specifically into theological knowledge that should have been beyond their capability as women and identified Mother Angélique as particularly susceptible to his influence. In her analysis of Zamet's text, Daniella Kostroun has noted that he structured the *Mémoire* in relation to Paul's Second Letter to Timothy to include Saint-Cyran under the category of those "who make their way into households and captivate silly women... who are always being instructed and can never arrive at a knowledge of the truth."[22] The *Mémoire* and responses written by defenders of the nuns also played a part in debates at the time over the intellectual and moral capabilities of women.[23] Thus, among the other accusations Zamet made against Saint-Cyran, Zamet used his willingness to provide and encourage such knowledge among women as evidence against him. He claimed that Saint-Cyran could have such an influence on the nuns because, as women, they were "naturally friends of change and novelty."[24] He emphasized in this text that, when speaking to Mother Angélique, he could tell that the claims she made about Augustine on grace and Paul on predestination were only based on what she had heard secondhand and "without any foundation."[25] He portrayed Angélique as one who took the little knowledge she had learned from Saint-Cyran to take on the role of teacher, specifically a teacher of theology—something that should have been beyond both the knowledge she had gained and her ability as a woman. He wrote,

> The abovementioned Marie-Angélique took such a liking for the discourses of the abbot and filled up so much on the spirit of them, that she spoke of nothing else except the primitive church, the canons, the customs of the first Christians, the councils, the Fathers—principally of Saint Augustine—that she discussed them even with women who were going to visit there, who did not care about them as an extraordinary conversation and useless for them.[26]

Zamet here contrasted Angélique with the visitors to the convent who, unlike Angélique, recognized the uselessness of such knowledge for them as women. Now, this portrayal of Angélique as obsessed with theological knowledge—especially that of the early church—and wanting to spread that knowledge to others contrasts with the portrayal of Angélique in her own writings. For example, in her autobiographical account of her reform, Angélique emphasized that she only wrote under obedience.[27] Based on hints about her from other sources, it is likely that the reality of Angélique's personality and desire for knowledge fell somewhere in between those two portrayals.

Because of this context, my research has questioned the use of the term *theologian* (or rather, *théologienne*) as applied to women in seventeenth-century France, and specifically as applied to the Port-Royal nuns. In this sense, my work resonates with Mary Daly's critique that "women have had the power of *naming* stolen from us. We have not been free to use our own power to name ourselves, the world, or God."[28] In part because of the view of women in that period and in part due to the controversy over Jansenism at Port-Royal, the nuns had the power of naming stolen from them. They were derisively mocked as *théologiennes* without anyone stopping to consider that their writings held great theological content and that they very much were *théologiennes*, in a positive sense. Also, we must note in all this that the lack of recognition given to the Port-Royal nuns as theologians is not exclusive to them, but remains a broader problem

Théologienne, Théologien, Theologian?

about the way we look at women who wrote religious texts throughout history.[29] I would like to therefore reclaim the Port-Royal nuns as *théologiennes* in this positive sense and identify them as models for women theologians today.

However, to do this with the Port-Royal nuns, we need to examine the way that the term *théologienne* was used in the seventeenth century. This provides a starting point for arguing that the nuns qualify as *théologiennes* even in their own era, not just retrospectively. Etymologically, our English word *theologian* came from Latin via French, but modern definitions focus more on a specialization aspect of the theologian, perhaps a nod to the development of academic theology. For example, the *Oxford English Dictionary* defines a theologian as "one who is versed in theology," but especially "one who makes a study or profession of theology,"[30] while in French *La Rousse* defines a theologian (in both masculine and feminine) as a "specialist in theology."[31] While there is some importance to this academic specialization, when we look at history we need to remember that not everyone had the same access to such specialization, and we cannot apply the contemporary academic understanding of theology to figures like the Port-Royal nuns when we consider if their work would lead us to count them as theologians.

Interestingly, dictionary definitions from the seventeenth century tend to include a reference to the term *théologienne* (female) in their definition of a *théologien* (male), but the implication is always that such a mythical creature as a female theologian does not actually exist. Antoine Furetière, the author of the *Dictionnaire universel*, published in 1690, defined a *théologien* (male) as, one "who knows theology, who teaches it, or who wrote about it" (*Qui sçait la Theologie, qui l'enseigne, ou qui en a escrit*).[32] So, according to Furetière, three things make someone a theologian: knowledge, teaching, or writing. He did include the feminine version of the word in his dictionary definition, but his example for the feminine term suggested that a *théologienne* might not actually exist. He wrote, "St. Bridget can pass for a great *théologienne*, she wrote two fine volumes of revelations."[33] Thus, although he included the feminine version of the noun in the definition, the example implies that women could not become theologians. St. Bridget is not a theologian but can *pass for* a theologian. Similarly, the 1694 *Dictionary of the French Academy* defined the term *théologien* only in the masculine as someone "who

45

knows theology."³⁴ The entry explained that the word "can be said in the feminine in speaking of a woman or of a girl who would know [*sçauroit*] or who would claim to know [*pretendroit sçavoir*] theology."³⁵ This difference in verb tenses is suggestive. While the male theologian knows theology, the female theologian is someone *would know*—in the conditional—or *would claim to know* theology. Again, the definition suggests that the author did not believe in the possibility of a female theologian. Some women might have claimed to know theology, but the use of that language and the conditional verb tense suggests that the author believed that these claims were not true and that the term *théologienne* had a derogatory implication of one claiming knowledge beyond their ability.

Unsurprisingly, although neither of the seventeenth-century definitions referred to the necessity of a university degree to qualify as a theologian, the male academics writing these dictionaries did not consider the existence of a female theologian as a possibility. There were, however, women like Angélique who did fulfill Furetière's criteria for a theologian, namely, one who knows, writes, and teaches theology.³⁶ As a nun, Angélique had access to education in theology—more education than would have been available to laywomen at this time.³⁷ This, of course, would not have been the same course of study as that offered at the universities of the day, but she learned theology through the education she received as a child, the reading of devotional texts, and the sermons of visiting preachers. And, furthermore, as abbess, she regularly gave discourses to the nuns at her convent, commenting on Scripture and texts such as the *Rule of Saint Benedict*, so she also fulfilled the criteria for teaching in theology.

Finally, the texts we have by Mother Angélique, such as her autobiographical account, show how she wrote theology. She wrote this account of her reform of the convent as part of a historiographical project to collect the writings of the nuns, spearheaded by her niece, Angélique de Saint-Jean Arnauld d'Andilly, and nephew, Antoine Le Maistre. Although both Angélique and Angélique de Saint-Jean emphasized that Angélique wrote this account under obedience, Angélique de Saint-Jean also commented how Angélique frequently spoke to the nuns of her desire to write a book on divine providence—that, "especially from all that had happened to her, she had reason to write a book on the providence of God."³⁸ The rhetoric

Théologienne, Théologien, Theologian?

of humility was common in monastic writing of this era, especially writings by women, so we can raise the question of whether or not this reluctance to write was genuine. Her account is ultimately a theological reflection on the presence and her understanding of divine providence throughout her life experiences in relation to Port-Royal.

Beyond that, however, she also employed in her text a sophisticated use of the genres of autohagiography and apology.[39] First, her account is modeled after the (auto)hagiographies of other women, employing certain characteristic themes and events to structure her life. For example, some common themes in accounts of the lives of other religious women include the rejection of marriage, a conflict with the woman's family, and a conversion experience. Angelique included all of these in the story of her life—the temptation from her Protestant relatives to leave the convent for marriage that she ultimately rejected, the conflict with her family over the reform of the convent that culminated in the "day of the grille," and her conversion based on the sermon about Christ's humility in the incarnation.

Angélique's account, however, is not just the story of her life, but also an apology for her reform and especially her choice of Saint-Cyran as a confessor. This appears particularly in the way that she wrote about her association with Francis de Sales in comparison to her association with Saint-Cyran. For example, in discussing her relationship with Francis de Sales, she wrote,

> If this holy man had remained in France, I believe that I would have taken great advantage from his holy direction, which was by no means soft and gentle, as the majority of the world imagined him, because he only revealed [that] to souls who had a true confidence in him and that he saw disposed to believe it. And of all those that I had seen before him, I found none of them as firm as him.[40]

At the time Angélique wrote her account, the church had not yet declared Francis de Sales a saint—his beatification would occur in 1661—but he had a great reputation in France and his process for canonization had begun immediately after his death in 1622. Since part of the accusations against Port-Royal and Jansenism came from their rigorism, she illustrated in this example how even Francis de

Approaching Theology

Sales supported that rigorist program. In contrast, when she wrote of Saint-Cyran in her account, she said,

> And it is necessary to remark that it was not that this holy man carried people through any force or constraint, in the spirit of penitence, nor that he ordered great mortifications and austerities. But God made for him the grace, by the strength of solid truths, to touch hearts greatly with the love and the respect that one owed to God. So, he made to emerge grief for having offended [God] and such a great desire to satisfy [God], that one always wanted to do more than he wanted.[41]

Here, we have a defense of the accusations of rigorism against Saint-Cyran, that he did not force people to perform harsher penances than others would require, but rather that God worked through him to inspire such austerities in others. Ultimately, Angélique wanted to consider Francis de Sales and Saint-Cyran as equals when it came to the question of rigorism. She made this explicit argument in a letter to Anne of Austria at the end of her life, arguing that Jeanne de Chantal had visited Port-Royal after she had introduced Saint-Cyran as their confessor, and that Chantal claimed that the life there conformed to the teachings of Francis de Sales.[42] What this shows is how Angélique did not just write about her spiritual experiences, but deliberately constructed her narrative in a way to make theological arguments. Other writings by the Port-Royal nuns, including some that were published at the time, deliberately portrayed the convent as conforming to the Tridentine reforms of religious life.[43] Thus, not just Angélique, but the other Port-Royal nuns as well, wrote texts that we could consider today as works of theology.

Furthermore, in writing these texts, the Port-Royal nuns redefined what it meant to do theology in a way that did not depend on the educational system of the university. As Kostroun has argued,

> Underlying the nuns' strategy was their understanding of the science of saints, which involved a belief that, when theologians taught the truth about religion, they did so equally through their words and through their actions. The science of saints meant that, even though the nuns

were barred from reading theological texts by the Church, they still could appropriate the truths within them by following the pious examples of their authors. By logical extension, when the nuns imitated the pious examples of saintly theologians, they too were communicating their theological truths.[44]

The strategy of the nuns was thus in direct contradiction to the dictionary definitions of theology of the time that indicated that women could not do or produce theology. This expansion of the understanding of theology means that we need to look differently at the work of women in history, such as with hagiographical texts, to effectively read them for their theological content and understand their authors as theologians.[45] By doing so, we can understand these women as having made a contribution to theology and acting as theologians according to the definitions of the time—that is, they both knew, taught, and wrote theology in their contexts.[46]

So why does all this matter? The lack of historical models of women as theologians can make it more difficult for women to self-identify in this way today, even with the academic credentials of theology that are now available to us as well as to men. As Ann Kirkus Wetherilt has argued, "Women, and others whose voices have been excluded from the 'authoritative' structures of white, western, masculinist theological thought, have never been entirely silenced, yet the cost has been, and is, great."[47] This is precisely why I see it so important to recover the voices of these women, like the Port-Royal nuns, as theologians.

Some theologians have done similar work to what I do with the Port-Royal nuns in the past. For example, Marie Anne Mayeski, also a historical theologian, has looked at examples of women theologians through the lens of hagiographical texts in the early medieval era.[48] Other feminist theologians have addressed this same issue, though not always explicitly connected to the idea of women as theologians and not explicitly from the methods of historical theology. Mary Catherine Hilkert's *Speaking with Authority* looks at Catherine of Siena as a model of hope and courage for women raising their voices in the church today. This is important because "in times that test our courage and hope, the memory of those who have gone before us in faith can sustain and empower us."[49] Although Hilkert does not identify herself as a historical theologian, she is using historical-theological methods, looking back at Catherine of Siena in context and, especially, arguing how she functions as a model today. As another example, Elizabeth Johnson's *Friends of God and Prophets* aims to recover the symbol of the communion of saints "in such a way that it itself functions in a befriending and prophetic way, nourishing women in the struggle for life and equal human dignity and nourishing the church through memory and hope into being a true community of the friends of God and prophets."[50] Although she does not identify her book explicitly as such, it is also an example of historical theology in that she is drawing on a combination of feminist historical research and practices of memory and her own feminist theological training to reclaim the idea of the saints for women. She notes early in the book that the issue is that those who have been identified as saints in the Catholic tradition have been primarily male, European, upper class, and clerics and that least represented are married women, "reflecting the dualistic assessment that to be female is a handicap, but to be a sexually active woman renders one almost incapable of embodying the sacred."[51] The problem she identifies—and that she aims to rectify with her work—is that the lack of female role models among the saints both suppresses the history of women's holiness and deprives women today of a sense of holiness in their own lives. Her work confronts the same problem faced by the feminist historical theologian, namely, that the historical record of women as saints has not been as well recorded as that of men primarily because men are most often the ones recording this history. This is in part why the Port-Royal nuns are so exceptional—namely, that they made a concerted effort to record their own history. Elisabeth Schüssler Fiorenza has a similar motive to Johnson in her book *In Memory of Her*, looking not at the tradition of saints, but at the women disciples as depicted in the New Testament and early Christian history, and aiming to reclaim this history for both women and men. She identifies this as important because "as long as the stories and history of women in the beginnings of Christianity are not theologically conceptualized as an integral part of the proclamation of the gospel, biblical texts and traditions formulated and codified by men will remain oppressive to women."[52] She too does not self-identify as a historical theologian, but her work explicitly draws on not only her biblical training, but also on historical methods and

Théologienne, Théologien, Theologian?

feminist theology. For her, the recovery of these stories can serve not only as a reclaiming of the past for women, but as a source of empowerment for women as well. For a nontheological example, in her memoir *Recollections of My Nonexistence*, Rebecca Solnit writes about her realization later in her life that she had

> grown up in a country where almost everything named after a person—mountains, rivers, towns, bridges, buildings, states, parks—was named after a man, and nearly all the statues were of men. Women were allegorical figures—liberty and justice—but not actual people. A landscape full of places named after women and statues of women might have encouraged me and other girls in profound ways. The names of women were absent, and these absences were absent from our imaginations. It was no wonder we were supposed to be so slender as to shade into nonexistence.[53]

In the end, representation matters.

This question about representation has influenced my own career as a theologian. I previously wrote a blog post about one of the formative influences on my theology career, Fr. James Walsh, SJ, who I had as a professor as an undergraduate.[54] He was a scholar of the Old Testament, but his method of studying texts—focusing closely on word choice and analyzing each sentence in detail—influenced the way that I later read Blaise Pascal's *Pensées*, which ultimately led to my study of Jansenism and the Port-Royal nuns and even the way that I teach students how to read theological texts today. Another major influence on my theological development was Fr. Thomas King, SJ, who was the professor I had for my required theology class in my first semester at Georgetown University, the class that led me to eventually declare a major in theology and pursue a career in academic theology.

Reflecting on my own experience I think I was hesitant to self-identify as a theologian for a long time in part because most of my role models for academic theology had not only been men, but priests. (Now, I should just note that I have had the opportunity to be mentored over the years by some excellent female theologians and historians, but as a historical theologian, many of my mentors over the years have been men.[55]) So this question of what makes a theologian in the seventeenth century isn't just an academic question for me, but also a personal one. I would venture that it has made a difference in my choices—especially when compared to my male undergraduate friends who also pursued careers in theology. Although we do not have good statistics on the number of women theologians, Mary Ann Hinsdale published some research in 2017 into the presence of women on doctoral faculties of theology.[56] Her research showed that, for example, there had not been a significant increase in the presence of women as members of the Catholic Theological Society of America between 2003 and 2017, and that there were still few women theologians in major Catholic faculties of theology. Because of this, many women theologians today were, like me, inspired to become theologians because of the examples of male undergraduate professors. I do think that has made a difference in the confidence I have had to speak out about my research. In a sense, because of my formation in theology, the power to name myself has been, maybe not stolen, but withheld from me in part because I couldn't identify myself with the life experiences of those who taught me how to be a theologian.

That said, I do see myself as a theologian today. I fulfill the contemporary understanding of an academic specialist in theology, and I do so from an Anselmian perspective of "faith seeking understanding." My historical-theological research into the Christian tradition through a feminist lens is rooted in a search for a greater understanding of my own faith. I am also one who fulfills the criteria of Furetière for a theologian. Namely, I know theology through the education that I received and the continued reading and study that I do constantly. I teach theology regularly, as I work currently at a teaching-focused institution where I teach students about the Christian tradition every semester. Finally, I also regularly write theology, both as a contributor to *Women in Theology* and in my other writing and research. Although Furetière's definition is not contemporary, understanding the development of the use of that term is instructive in thinking about who we name as theologians today and whether, as Daly's work suggests, we claim the power to name ourselves as such.

NOTES

1. This chapter is an expanded version of my post "Théologienne, Théologien, Theologian? From Angélique Arnauld to Mary

Théologienne, Théologien, Theologian? Daly," *WIT: Women in Theology,* February 16, 2016, https://womenintheology.org/2016/02/16/theologienne-theologien-theologian-from-angelique-arnauld-to-mary-daly/.

2. Mary Daly, *Beyond God the Father: Toward a Philosophy of Women's Liberation* (Boston: Beacon Press, 1985).

3. Daly, *Beyond God the Father,* 4.

4. Patrick Carey, "History and Theology: A Personal Confession," *U.S. Catholic Historian* 23, no. 2 (2005): 11.

5. Pontifical Council for Justice and Peace, *Compendium of the Social Doctrine of the Church* (Washington, DC: USCCB Publishing, 2005), §144. For similar methodological arguments, see Elizabeth A. Johnson, *She Who Is: The Mystery of God in Feminist Theological Discourse,* tenth anniversary ed. (New York: Crossroad, 2002), 30–31; Rosemary Radford Ruether, *Sexism and God-Talk: Toward a Feminist Theology* (Boston: Beacon Press, 1993), 18–19.

6. *Compendium,* §144.

7. *Compendium,* §145, 295.

8. *Compendium,* §146–47; see also §224 in the context of marriage and family.

9. *Compendium,* §147.

10. I take inspiration in my methods from the feminist recovery of women in the New Testament and early church by Elisabeth Schüssler Fiorenza, *In Memory of Her: A Feminist Theological Reconstruction of Christian Origins,* tenth anniversary ed. (New York: Crossroad, 1994). See Elissa Cutter, "Toward a Feminist Historical Theology: Part II, Feminist Biblical Interpretation," *WIT: Women in Theology,* October 27, 2021, https://womenintheology.org/2021/10/27/toward-a-feminist-historical-theology-part-ii-feminist-biblical-interpretation/.

11. For information about Angélique and the Port-Royal nuns in English, see John J. Conley, *Adoration and Annihilation: The Convent Philosophy of Port-Royal* (South Bend, IN: University of Notre Dame Press, 2009); Daniella Kostroun, *Feminism, Absolutism, and Jansenism: Louis XIV and the Port-Royal Nuns* (Cambridge: Cambridge University Press, 2011); Alexander Sedgwick, *The Travails of Conscience: The Arnauld Family and the Ancien Régime* (Cambridge, MA: Harvard University Press, 1998); and F. Ellen Weaver, *The Evolution of the Reform of Port-Royal: From the Rule of Cîteaux to Jansenism* (Paris: Beauchesne, 1978).

12. Elissa Cutter, "Monastic Reform in Seventeenth-Century France: The Cistercian and Tridentine Influences on Angélique Arnauld's Reform of the Convent of Port-Royal," *Cistercian Studies Quarterly* 52, no. 4 (2017): 425–51; and Weaver, *The Evolution of the Reform of Port-Royal*.

13. Elissa Cutter, "Modern-Day Jansenism?" *WIT: Women in Theology*, October 1, 2014, https://womenintheology.org/2014/10/01/modern-day-jansenism/.

14. As quoted in Kostroun, *Feminism, Absolutism, and Jansenism*, 92.

15. Conley, *Adoration and Annihilation*, 27.

16. Louis Fontaines [Zacharie de Lisieux], *Relation du pays de Jansenie* (Rouen, 1693), 22. All translations from French are my own unless cited from another source.

17. Antoine Furetière, *Dictionnaire universel* (The Hague, 1690), s.v. "Quenouille."

18. Jean de Brisacier, *Le Jansenisme confondu dans l'advocat du Sr. Callaghan* (Paris, 1651). The foreword of this text has unnumbered pages and the other references I make in this chapter are to the same section of the text.

19. Virginia Burrus, "The Heretical Woman as Symbol in Alexander, Athansius, Epiphanius, and Jerome," *The Harvard Theological Review* 84, no. 3 (1991): 229–48.

20. See Burrus, "The Heretical Woman as Symbol," 244.

21. See 1 Cor 14:34–35.

22. 2 Tim 3:6–7.

23. Kostroun, *Feminism, Absolutism, and Jansenism*, 34–38.

24. Sébastien Zamet, *Mémoire*, in *Les premières controverses jansénistes en France (1640–1649)*, by Albert de Meyer (Louvain: J. van Linthout, 1917), 493.

25. Zamet, *Mémoire*, 494.

26. Zamet, *Mémoire*, 493–94.

27. Angélique Arnauld, *Relation de la Mère Angélique Arnauld*, ed. Jean Lesaulnier, *Chroniques de Port-Royal* 41 (1992): 11.

28. Daly, *Beyond God the Father*, 8.

29. Andrew Prevot, "No Mere Spirituality: Recovering a Tradition of Women Theologians," *Journal of Feminist Studies in Religion* 33, no. 1 (2007): 107–17. See also my short critiques: "No 'Church Mothers'? That Seems Doubtful," *WIT: Women in Theology*, April 22,

Théologienne, Théologien, Theologian?

2016, https://womenintheology.org/2016/04/22/no-church-mothers-that-seems-doubtful/; "No Church Mothers: Part II," *WIT: Women in Theology,* February 10, 2017, https://womenintheology.org/2017/02/10/no-church-mothers-part-ii/; and "No Church Mothers: Part III, Theology vs. Spirituality," *WIT: Women in Theology,* May 10, 2022, https://womenintheology.org/2022/05/10/no-church-mothers-part-iii-theology-vs-spirituality/.

30. "Theologian, n," *OED Online,* June 2022, Oxford University Press, https://www.oed.com/.

31. "Théologien, théologienne," *La Rousse,* https://www.larousse.fr/dictionnaires/francais/théologien/77719.

32. Furetière, *Dictionnaire universel,* s.v. "Théologien, enne."

33. Furetière, "Théologien, enne."

34. *Dictionnaire de l'Académie française,* 1st ed. (Paris, 1694), s.v. "Théologien," http://artfl.atilf.fr/dictionnaires/ACADEMIE/PREMIERE/premiere.fr.html.

35. *Dictionnaire de l'Académie française,* s.v. "Théologien."

36. Furetière, "Théologien, enne." For more on this argument, see Elissa Cutter, "The Early Modern Abbess as *Théologienne*: The Theology and Spirituality of Mother Angélique Arnauld" (PhD diss., Saint Louis University, 2016).

37. Conley, *Adoration and Annihilation,* 3; Silvia Evangelisti, *Nuns: A History of Convent Life, 1450–1700* (Oxford: Oxford University Press, 2007), 70.

38. Arnauld, *Relation,* 10.

39. Elissa Cutter, "Apology in the Form of Autohagiography: Angélique Arnauld's Defense of Her Reform of Port-Royal," *Catholic Historical Review* 105, no. 2 (2019): 275–303.

40. Arnauld, *Relation,* 42.

41. Arnauld, *Relation,* 61–62.

42. Angélique Arnauld, "Lettre 1607 à la reine mère Anne d'Autriche, 25 mai 1661," in *Œuvres complètes,* t. I, v. III, Lettres, ed. Jean Lesaulnier, Françoise Pouge-Bellais, and Anne-Claire Volongo, Univers Port-Royal 41 (Paris: Classiques Garnier, 2020), 2459.

43. Conley, *Adoration and Annihilation,* 15.

44. Kostroun, *Feminism, Absolutism, and Jansenism,* 240.

45. Marie Anne Mayeski, *Women at the Table: Three Medieval Theologians* (Collegeville, MN: Liturgical Press, 2004), 1–11.

46. Furetière, "Théologien, enne."

47. Ann Kirkus Wetherilt, *That They May Be Many: Voices of Women, Echoes of God* (New York: Continuum, 1994), 43.

48. Mayeski, *Women at the Table*.

49. Mary Catherine Hilkert, *Speaking with Authority: Catherine of Siena and the Voices of Women Today* (Mahwah, NJ: Paulist Press, 2008), 13.

50. Elizabeth A. Johnson, *Friends of God and Prophets: A Feminist Theological Reading of the Communion of Saints* (New York: Continuum, 1998), 3.

51. Johnson, *Friends of God and Prophets*, 27–28.

52. Schüssler Fiorenza, *In Memory of Her*, xlv.

53. Rebecca Solnit, *Recollections of My Nonexistence: A Memoir* (Penguin Books, 2020), 87, Kindle.

54. Elissa Cutter, "'For it is not to be doubted that the duration of this life is but a moment; that the state of death is eternal, whatever may be its nature,'" *WIT: Women in Theology*, July 7, 2015, https://womenintheology.org/2015/07/07/the-duration-of-this-life-is-but-a-moment/.

55. Elissa Cutter, "Why I Write for *WIT*: The Gender Disparity of Historical Theology," *WIT: Women in Theology*, May 31, 2019, https://womenintheology.org/2019/05/31/why-i-write-for-wit-the-gender-disparity-of-historical-theology/.

56. Mary Ann Hinsdale, "Who Are the 'Begats'? Or Women Theologians Shaping Women Theologians," *Journal of Feminist Studies in Religion* 33, no. 1 (2017): 91–106.

5

UNPACKING "BIBLICAL WOMANHOOD"

Theological Nostalgia, Gender, and History

Allison Murray

Introduction

All our theologies have a history. As someone who has trained as a historian within the broader discipline of theological studies, I am interested in both the histories of particular Christian doctrines and communities *and* how history serves as a theological resource. Understanding our orientation to the past is an important aspect of theological reflection and self-awareness. In the words of former Archbishop of Canterbury Rowan Williams, "Good theology does not come from bad history."[1] This chapter will look at a theological paradigm known as *complementarianism*, specifically focusing on how ideas about history function within it. In my view this paradigm is a glaring example of bad history begetting bad theology. I take issue with the narrowness and heavy prescriptiveness of complementarianism on many levels

Approaching Theology

as a Christian, a feminist, an academic trained in the disciplines of history and theology, and someone who believes in the full humanity and goodness of LGBTQ+ persons. What follows is one of (several possible) theohistorical critiques of this position, which serves in turn as an invitation to theologians of all stripes (both the everyday and the academic) to consider historical literacy as a necessary component of good theological reflection.

Complementarianism

In the later decades of the twentieth century, to counter "second wave" feminist ideas about gender being the product of socialization, antifeminist evangelicals in America began promoting a particular gendered theological anthropology they named "biblical manhood and womanhood." Teachings on "biblical manhood and womanhood" started popping up in evangelical trade books in the 1970s. By the late 1980s they were more systematically articulated under the banner of complementarianism by organizations such as the Council on Biblical Manhood and Womanhood (CBMW), which was established in 1987. While there are overlapping elements with Roman Catholic notions of gender complementarity, these evangelical Protestant expressions of complementarian theological anthropology evolved independently.[2] The evangelical complementarian theological paradigm understands male and female persons as "ontologically equal," yet "functionally different."[3] Within this mode of theological anthropology, manhood and womanhood are innate, divinely ordained categories of identity.

To accompany these fixed identities, proponents of "biblical manhood and womanhood" understand that men and women have been given distinct roles in the church, the home, and society "ordained by God as part of the created order," that "should find an echo in every human heart."[4] These distinct roles place men in positions of leadership and authority and call women to submit and follow. The way these roles are thought to "complement" one another is the source of the paradigm's name. Complementarianism has spread through the work of the CBMW, sermons, radio programs, conferences, and (of most interest to the current discussion) through books written for lay evangelical audiences. Books presenting "biblical manhood and womanhood" as gospel have abounded in the evangelical trade market after beginning slowly in the 1970s and building to an outright boom in the 1990s and early 2000s. It is these texts that serve as the basis for this analysis of complementarian teachings. Within these books, complementarians have offered readers a complete gender paradigm on which they can build their lives, base their family arrangements, and ensure the purity, health, and maintenance of their faith communities and their nation.

"Biblical manhood and womanhood" (BMW) are, of course, linked to a particular reading of the Bible, which serves as the ultimate authority for believers within the large tent of evangelicalism. There are three biblical texts that feature particularly in complementarian writings: Genesis 1–3, Ephesians 5, and Proverbs 31. This set of biblical texts makes up what I call the "complementarian micro-canon," and while other sections of Scripture do appear with some regularity, these texts are the most frequently analyzed and interpreted by complementarian authors to support their views. While the Bible does play a large role in complementarian discourse, complementarian authors draw on more than *sola scriptura*. Looking at extrabiblical argumentation put forward in support for "biblical womanhood," one finds a great deal of nostalgia-based rhetoric posing as historical fact. This nostalgic pattern presents ahistorical perspectives on gender and family life and gives these a theological gloss, presenting the past as holier, homogenous, and idyllic—the "better-before." These appeals to "history" serve to legitimize the properness and rightness of "biblical" gender roles and, less directly, to hide the privileging of certain class and racial identities within the complementarian framework.

Complementarian Portrayal of the Past

As a rule, complementarian authors assume that better practices and values existed in the past. They tend to support arguments for BMW and its accompanying prescriptions with references to "the way things used to be." Whether it is how faithful Christians should understand themselves, how a Christian family should arrange itself in the home, or how to embody a biblically sanctioned sexuality, the past—not the present—serves as the best exemplar for complementarian authors. It is something that needs to be reclaimed, renewed, or retrieved. In the complementarian historical narrative, contemporary society has moved people away from healthy, accurate assessments of masculine and feminine identity and purpose. As Mary Kassian explained to her readers in 2005's *The Feminist Mistake*,

> Up until the middle of the last century, Western culture as a whole generally embraced a Judeo-Christian perspective on gender, sexuality, and the purpose and structure of the family....Differences between male and female were accepted and seldom questioned....Individuals had a sense of what it meant to be a man or a woman and the appropriate outworking of gender roles and relationships.[5]

Since then, gendered confusion and chaos have reigned, the reader is told, which have contributed to societal instability and the weaker witness of the gospel in the contemporary environment.

We see complementarian authors reaching back to different points in the past when discussing the ideal Christian home, sometimes relying on the recent past of their own childhoods and at other points reaching back centuries. Susan Hunt and Jim George both reference the Puritans who began the colonial settlement of America as good examples of "the *original* American dream."[6] Carolyn McCulley draws on the notion of Republican Motherhood, "the golden age of domesticity," as a past exemplar for contemporary women.[7] Additionally, McCulley, along with Donna Otto and Steve Farrar, positions the Industrial Revolution as the watershed event that disrupted patterns that created healthy homes and families. In contemporary times, according to Farrar's 1993 book *Point Man: How a Man Can Lead His Family*, "Those seeds are bearing fruit. And the fruit is killing us."[8]

Farrar's alarmist message about the present casts the past in a golden light. He paints a uniform picture of the past, where self-sufficient pre-Industrial families engendered healthy masculinity and femininity in their children through gender-segregated working patterns at home. According to Farrar, "the pattern remained the same as it had for centuries," and pre-Industrial fathers "raised their boys and as a result there was tremendous stability in the family," because its members "were together nearly every waking hour."[9] His portrayal of the past is homey and idyllic. Predictable patterns of gender-segregated at-home training led to social stability. Notably absent from his historical portrait: war, famine, untimely deaths due to accident or disease, social stratification, chattel slavery, children sent to other families to work in service or as apprentices, or any other fact of life that might lead to turbulence or difficulty. Farrar assumes the patterns and rhythms of the healthiest, most privileged, Anglo settler class applied to everyone in colonial America (not to mention all of history up to that point). The nuanced realities of the past are not important to Farrar. Instead, his priority is to construct a picture of a homogenous, stable past from which his readers should uniformly draw inspiration on how to structure family life today.

The Better-Before

Consistently, the dominant historical orientation of complementarian authors is informed by a sense that the best things were in the past and that a return to these values and rhythms is an important requisite for future prosperity. It is common for conservative movements to imagine some sort of golden age where people were protected from the problems and fears of the present by better values and social structures. In this way complementarianism is a quintessentially conservative movement, with its hope for a bright future tied to recovering the warm golden glow of the way things "used to be," in the amorphous and unspecific past I call the "better-before." I use this term to distinguish between the actual past (as much as we can know it through historical inquiry) and the rhetorical "past" employed by complementarians. The better-before has no specific time frame, geographic, racial, or socioeconomic location. The details about "better"—such as where, for whom, how, and why—are not part of the formulation. One need only conjure or project an image of the past offered in a lament of contrast to the present. For another example, we can turn to *What He Must Be...If He Wants to Marry My Daughter*, a 2009 book by pastor and author Voddie Baucham Jr. He opens a chapter of his book with the 1828 Webster's Dictionary definition of *patriarch*. After informing readers that this refers to "the father and ruler of a family; one who governs by paternal right... usually applied to the progenitors of the Israelites," Baucham then quotes the following:

> Anyone interested in improving relations between men and women today and tomorrow must proceed by taking a page from yesterday. For today's tale regarding manhood and womanhood is, alas, both too brief and hardly edifying.[10]

Typical of complementarian construals of the past/present divide, these statements directly contrast the absurd, inferior, hardly edifying present with the better-before, revealing the openly nostalgic character of the BMW way of life.

Appeals to the better-before serve a specific rhetorical and discursive function in complementarian advice. Primarily, as authors invite their readers to identity with (or hope for the restoration of) the better-before, these appeals to "the past" serve to sever readers' identification with their contemporary environment. By aligning with the better-before instead of the present, complementarian authors present a means by which their readers can psychologically differentiate themselves from their surrounding culture. Adherence to complementarian views is one way that biblical men and women can locate themselves within that narrative of difference and shore up their own sense of identity as dedicated, orthodox, evangelical Christians.

The Nostalgia Trap

Comparing complementarian authors' notions of "the past" to secondary literature on the various historical periods to which they appeal reveals significant gaps between authors' notions and historical realities. As historian of gender and families Mona Gleason notes, research into twentieth-century family life has "reinforced our understanding that familial experience varied across gender, class, ethnicity, time, and place and was shaped by external and internal forces." And even if there was a central "notion of a stable, 'normal' family...a static, one-dimensional 'traditional family' has never existed."[11] Complementarians' views about where individuals, families, and society should be headed are informed by inferred values from a homogeneous past that never was.

These appeals to the better-before are more rhetorically nostalgic than they are historical. This use of an imprecise sense of the past in envisioning the future has been analyzed and explored by family historian Stephanie Coontz. Out of her research on the historical realities of American family life, Coontz coined the term "the nostalgia trap" as a way of describing the way ideas about the better-before can impact individuals' and governments' postures toward societal change. Her 1992 monograph *The Way We Never Were* explores common better-before-informed myths (such as American self-sufficiency, the breadwinning husband, and the stay-at-home mother) and exposes the significant gaps between these myths and how American families actually operated in the retrievable past. In the preface to the 2016 rerelease of *The Way We Never Were*, Coontz notes that while many things had changed since she first published the book, "the tendency for many Americans to view present-day family and gender relations through the foggy lens of nostalgia for a mostly mythical past," has remained constant. She continues,

> Nostalgia is a very human trait....As time passes, the actual complexity of our history—even of our own personal experience—gets buried under the weight of the ideal image. Selective memory is not a bad thing when it leads children to forget the arguments in the back seat of the car [on a summer holiday] and to look forward to their next vacation. But it's a serious problem when it leads grown-ups to try to recreate a past that either never existed at all or whose seemingly attractive features were inextricably linked to injustices and restrictions on liberty that few Americans would tolerate today.[12]

In order to move forward helpfully, Coontz suggests that American lawmakers "need to get past abstract nostalgia for traditional family values and develop a clearer sense of how past families actually worked....Good history and responsible social policy should help people incorporate the full complexity and the trade-offs of family change into their analyses and thus into action. Mythmaking does not accomplish this end."[13] In other words, legislators and policy makers need to beware this nostalgia trap as they pursue their work to properly take the demands of reality into account.

The Problems of a Theological Nostalgia Trap

Just as Coontz expressed concern at the impact the nostalgia trap has had on American domestic policies, I would raise concern over the preoccupation with the better-before in "biblical manhood and womanhood" discourse. Within the complementarian framework, "the past" is not a real place. It is a screen upon which nostalgic memories, grandmother's anecdotes, and distrust of the present can project themselves, intermingled, to provide a sense of what can be achieved if everyone were to follow their rules. There is no robust acknowledgement of socioeconomic structures, class differentiation, systemic racism, ethnic diversity, or other social factors that have impacted human families throughout history (American or otherwise). Rather than understanding the past and all its complexities, the better-before is portrayed as a homogenous mass where consensus and uniformity reigned.

One of the ways this oversimplification shows up is in how appeals to the past are (or, in many cases, are not) supported by references and footnotes. Within complementarian books appeals to the past are usually both sweeping and underresearched. Where readers will typically find extensive referencing and footnotes to accompany complementarians' claims argued from Scripture, similar supports are absent with most historical assertions. Arguments based on the better-before are typically plainly stated as matters-of-fact, with no external sources provided to support or corroborate the authors' claims. Where any references are to be found they typically lead to sources that are some combination of broad, shallow, outdated, and insufficient to support the claims being made. This is the case even among the more academically qualified complementarian authors, such as Steve Farrar. Let us consider Farrar's homogenized and idyllic pronouncements about pre-Industrial American family life in *Point Man* mentioned above. The source for his historical arguments? An

Unpacking "Biblical Womanhood"

encyclopedia entry that was already nearly forty years old when his book went to print.[14] We can also look to 2008's *The New Eve* written by Robert Lewis. Lewis tells readers about another time in history when women gained more legal rights, started pursuing careers more intently, and started having fewer children. The time and place: Rome in the second century. The heading on the page reads "A Warning from History"—as he reminds readers that Rome fell shortly after this "new woman" appeared on the scene.[15] Early Rome had a consensus, changing gender norms caused a fracture, and chaos resulted. Lewis pulls support for his consensus-fracture-chaos narrative from very small sections of Will Durant's 1944 *Caesar & Christ*, a sweeping narrative history that touches on gendered elements of Roman life only in throwaway, undocumented comments that are not linked to the collapse of the empire. Lewis uses references to Durant's work to support causal arguments Durant never made.

While some might dismiss this complaint as a theologically minded historian expecting too much from nonhistorians, such a dismissal ignores the degree to which complementarian authors appeal to the past to support their arguments. Noting the texts' lack of historicity and historical accuracy is important because it demonstrates the extrabiblical elements of these authors' worldview that inform their perspectives, and, in turn, how they direct their readers to operate within the world. If this was merely an argument about the interpretation of Ephesians 5 or Genesis 3, appeals to the past would be unnecessary. The prominence of the better-before in complementarianism demonstrates how integral ahistoricity is to this gender paradigm. Complementarians have a homogenized misconception of what the past looked like, and they use this false picture as a model for the present and future. Their lack of nuance for understanding varied realities of the past bleeds into a lack of nuance in understanding the people of the present as well.

In appealing to "history" to make their discursive claims they dehistoricize the inherently historical and contextual Christian faith. The force and impact of the nostalgia trap is additionally problematic when theological imperatives are added to the discourse. Complementarian authors give copious advice on how to consider individual identity, marriage, parenting, housekeeping, and sexual intimacy in light of "biblical" gendered mandates. Men should provide, women should stay home; mothers should be soft and caring, fathers should discipline; husbands "require" frequent sexual satisfaction from their wives, wives need emotional support and attention; and so on. Much of the advice and prescriptions present intragender uniformity as a given. Very little considers an audience that may inhabit different cultural or socioeconomic positions than the authors do themselves. Writers tend to assume that their advice is equally applicable to all their potential readers. Despite practical limitations that render their advice untenable in many circumstances (singleness, childlessness, families with two working parents—let alone queerness, multigenerational households, diverse strengths, individual temperaments, and so on), these authors routinely insist that their approach to the Christian life is the best, even only, approach worthy of the name. Readers of complementarian books are told they can please God by performing a set of gender roles that are culturally, temporally, and class bound. The authors' advice has a high likelihood of excluding and alienating many believers, reinforcing unjust social patterns, and adding spiritual anxieties to marginalization that may already be taking place owing to racial, ethnic, and socioeconomic inequalities. More plainly said, when authors suggest that all Christians must arrange life along complementarian values informed by the better-before while ignoring the greater social, cultural, and economic forces that made the ideal past a reality for the very specific few, they are setting readers up for failure and disillusionment. The authors' default nostalgia demonstrates their own failure to wrestle with the complex interactions between gospel and culture over time. In attempting to universally mandate culture-bound particulars they undermine the universality of the gospel call by restricting faithfulness to those who are white, cis, straight, (upper) middle-class, married, parents.

Historically Literate Theological Inquiry

Complementarian authors are a glaring example of how nostalgia and a lack of historical literacy negatively affects the articulation of Christian thought and values. Good theology, like good social policy, cannot come from bad history. By this I do not mean to suggest

Unpacking "Biblical Womanhood"

that every pastor, theologian, and believer need run to the archives to be a faithful Christian. But I *do* think that bringing a certain sense of historical literacy and curiosity into our engagement with theological texts and spiritual advice books can help us approach both the gospel and the world with more awareness and humility. First, knowing a bit more about the past can help us to spot nostalgia and the better-before as it arises in our faith communities, in sermons and homilies, and in our reading of news, Christian books, etc. When those, à la Farrar, seek to alarm by comparing the present to a uniform and idyllic past, some historical awareness can help engender some calming skepticism. The challenges of our contemporary world are legion (and, frankly, enough to be getting on with) without the added pressure of nostalgic alarmism. Being aware of change and continuity through the course of history can help us to better understand both the particularity of our own circumstances and the commonalities we share with those who came before us. Asserting that a golden age existed where life was imbued with frictionless ease denies the realities of the past. Human life has forever been complex. No particular family arrangement can insulate all people from stress, struggles, or disillusionment.

Some working knowledge of the history of the Christian faith can help, too. Grappling with the interactions between gospel and culture has been an ever-present thread within the Christian tradition. Different cultures and societies have molded Christian teachings to their context and molded their cultures to Christian teachings in different ways. Complementarian authors will frequently position their advice as *the* Christian way. It is *a* Christian way informed by the values, hierarchies, and economy of the post–WWII white middle-class America. In knowing more about the ways Christians and church institutions have changed (and stayed the same) through time, we can develop a better appreciation for the internal diversity of our tradition. We can better recognize the diversity of the historic and contemporary church and the diverse ways the gospel applies to life, rather than maintaining a narrow ahistorical view. We don't all need to get PhDs in Christian history, but I do think knowing the stories of churches and Christians in historical and cultural contexts other than our own can be of immense value.

If you have never heard of complementarianism before it might be tempting to think that these are fringe views that fall somewhere on a spectrum of "interesting" to "distressing," but are irrelevant and distant. However fringe the opinions might seem to you, they are still worth attending to.[16] To borrow from priest and theologian Emily Hunter McGowin, the margins of a culture ultimately reflect the reality of the center, just in more glaring ways.[17] Dynamics within complementarianism—including the tendency to promote theological nostalgia—are unlikely to be constrained to the evangelical tent. This became glaringly obvious in the text of the American Supreme Court's *Dobbs v. Jackson Women's Health Organization* decision in June 2022, where cultural progress and innovation were contrasted with the pristine "deeply rooted traditions" of the nation's constitution. Nostalgic understanding of the nation's past served as a justification to dictate the "right" actions of the present. The impulse to allow the better-before to hold authority that I noticed among the evangelical authors I read is not unique to them. Whether or not we have been immersed in evangelical spaces it behooves us all to stop and consider how we have encountered (or promoted) nostalgia in our theological communities.

NOTES

1. Rowan Williams, *Why Study the Past? The Quest for the Historical Church* (Grand Rapids, MI: Eerdmans, 2005).

2. For more on the evolving notion of complementarity in the Roman Catholic tradition see Prudence Allen, *The Concept of Woman*, vol. 3, *The Search for Communion of Persons, 1500–2015* (Grand Rapids, MI: Eerdmans, 2017).

3. J. Lingon Duncan and Randy Stinson, "Preface (2006)," in *Recovering Biblical Manhood and Womanhood: A Response to Evangelical Feminism*, ed. Wayne Grudem and John Piper (Wheaton, IL: Crossway Books, 2006), 36.

4. Wayne Grudem and John Piper, eds., *Recovering Biblical Manhood and Womanhood: A Response to Evangelical Feminism* (Wheaton, IL: Crossway Books, 2006), 478.

5. Mary A. Kassian, *The Feminist Mistake: The Radical Impact of Feminism on Church and Culture* (Wheaton, IL: Crossway Books, 2005), 7–8.

6. Susan Hunt, *By Design: God's Distinctive Calling for Women* (Franklin, TN: Legacy Communications, 1994), 119. Emphasis original.

7. Carolyn McCulley, *Radical Womanhood: Feminine Faith in a Feminist World* (Chicago: Moody Publishers, 2008), 106.

8. Steve Farrar, *Point Man: How a Man Can Lead His Family*, updated ed. (Sisters, OR: Multnomah Books, 2003), 40. See also Donna Otto, *The Stay at Home Mom: For Women at Home and Those Who Want to Be* (Eugene, OR: Harvest House Publishers, 1997), 155–56.

9. Farrar, *Point Man*, 39.

10. Amy A. Kass and Leon R. Kass, "Proposing Courtship," *First Things*, October 1999, 32–41, as quoted in Voddie Baucham, *What He Must Be...If He Wants to Marry My Daughter* (Wheaton, IL: Crossway Books, 2009), 47–48.

11. Mona Lee Gleason, *Normalizing the Ideal: Psychology, Schooling, and the Family in Postwar Canada*, Studies in Gender and History (Toronto: University of Toronto Press, 1999), 11.

12. Stephanie Coontz, *The Way We Never Were: American Families and the Nostalgia Trap* (New York: Basic Books, 2016), 14.

13. Coontz, *The Way We Never Were*, 53.

14. Farrar, *Point Man*, 39.

15. Robert M. Lewis, *The New Eve: Choosing God's Best for Your Life* (Nashville: B&H Publishing, 2008), 11.

16. See, for example, the chapter "Unholy Trinity: Incel Ideology, Complementarian Theology, and Toxic Masculinity," in this volume by Alexandria Barbera and me.

17. Emily Hunter McGowin, *Quivering Families: The Quiverfull Movement and Evangelical Theology of the Family* (Minneapolis: Fortress Press, 2018), xxiv.

6

GOD OF MY ANCESTORS

A Filipina American Catholic's Reflection on Decolonizing Her Faith

Jessica Gapasin Dennis

Introduction

Several lifetimes ago, when my day job involved training catechists and working with adults in the RCIA (Rite of Christian Initiation for Adults), there was a metaphor I loved to use whenever I taught about the Mass. It's the one that compares the eucharistic celebration to a special family gathering: the Liturgy of the Word is when where we're sitting around catching up, telling the same old stories about our family; the Liturgy of the Eucharist is the part when we set the table and gather around it to share a meal. And in this sacred retelling of our stories, in the breaking of bread, we remember who we are as children of God, as brothers and sisters in Christ, and in doing so we deepen our identity as the body of Christ.

I have returned to this image often, especially as I've grappled with issues of identity and belonging as a second-generation Filipina American in the Catholic Church. My questions and general disquiet first started bubbling to the surface when I was in grad school, doing research about the introduction of the Christian faith to the Philippines:

> *What are the implications when the faith that I inherited is one that first came to my ancestors through force and colonial oppression?*
>
> *How do I understand my own identity and inherent dignity when the arrival of the Christian faith to the islands involved the stripping away of names and the taking of land?*
>
> *How do I reconcile the cognitive dissonance of loving Christ deeply and the awareness that my ancestors likely suffered at the hands of Christians?*

The Philippines has known close to four hundred years of colonization: over three hundred years under Spanish colonial rule (1565–1898) and then almost fifty years as a U.S. colony (1898–1946). While almost eighty years have passed since the Philippines gained its independence, the trauma of colonization is something that continues to have a ripple effect across generations. As Poka Laenui puts it, "Colonization and decolonization are social processes even more than they are political processes."[1] Long after the conquering nation has uprooted itself physically from the land, the aftermath of the mental, spiritual, and emotional harm caused by colonization is a wound that continues to fester.

In recent years, as more has been studied and written about the Filipino American experience, the term *colonial mentality* has been used to describe the effects of colonization on the mental health and psychological well-being of Filipino Americans and other populations who have known historical colonialism. Briefly defined, colonial mentality is "a condition in which the oppressed perceives oneself as inferior to the oppressor."[2] For Filipinos and Filipino Americans specifically, colonial mentality is "characterized by a perception of ethnic or cultural inferiority that is…a specific consequence of centuries of colonization under Spain and the U.S."[3] It "involves an automatic and uncritical rejection of anything Filipino and an automatic uncritical preference for anything American."[4] Colonial mentality is cited "as a major reason for the lack of societal presence, political clout, and social unity of the Filipino American community, and the lack of cultural pride, historical knowledge, and cultural appreciation among Filipino and Filipino American individuals."[5] In studies of Filipino American mental health, colonial mentality can be linked to "lower levels of self-esteem and more depression symptoms."[6]

Reflecting on my experience growing up in northern California, it's hard to unsee the insidiousness of colonial mentality in my own life. Throughout my childhood, my immigrant parents' expectations were implicit but clear: don't do anything to stick out or look different. The goal was to assimilate to the dominant American culture. A nursery rhyme I remember hearing frequently as a child went, *Sit down, sit down, you're rocking the boat.*

When we started at a new school, we were told that if asked, only English was spoken in the house (even though we heard at least three Filipino dialects on a regular basis). Comments about who was considered pretty and attractive were par for the course: people who were skinny and had small feet, who were light-skinned or had bridges in their noses (versus the more typical flat-nosed Filipinos)—all qualities that I did not possess. I have a distinct memory of putting a clothespin on my nose when I was eight years old because I was told it would make my nose pointier (it didn't work).

As a student at a predominantly white high school, I remember how uneasy and embarrassed I would feel when I saw another Filipino student being unabashedly proud of their Filipino heritage. Not only was I indifferent when it came to learning about Filipino history, I actively avoided joining any Filipino American organizations as a college student because I wrote them off as attention-seeking and unnecessary. If you were to ask my twenty-year-old self her opinion on Philippine independence, she would have genuinely been confused as to why the Philippines *wouldn't* want the benefits of being a U.S. territory.

It's truly mind-boggling how much clarity a person can gain with time and reflection. Only in hindsight am I able to recognize how steeped my worldview and self-worth was in colonial mentality. This recognition, this naming of colonial mentality as part of my history, along with my research of the Catholic Church's history in the Philippines, has helped me sort through and make meaning of my own experience as a Filipina American Catholic. Moreover, in the act of naming the injustice of colonization at the hands of the Catholic Church as part of my history I also (unbeknownst to me at the time) began paving the way for my own decolonization, a process that I am still in the thick of, and that I imagine will be in for some time.

As I engage in this process of decolonization, I've found the frameworks proposed by Poka Laenui[7] and Leny Strobel[8] to be particularly helpful in understanding my experience. Below is a hybrid of both frameworks, with both descriptive and prescriptive elements, which I will apply to describe and reflect on my own decolonization. In the same vein as Laenui, I would also emphasize that the first three phases are not meant to describe explicit stages where one graduates from one to the next. We might instead consider them spaces that all exist within a person, and that we tend to inhabit certain spaces, some at the same time and in various combinations, in particular seasons of our life. The last phase, Commitment and Action, is taken from Leny Strobel's framework and is mentioned here briefly as a prescriptive action for those who are looking for next steps in their own decolonization.

1. *Recovery and Discovery*—acquisition of historical and cultural knowledge.[9]
2. *Mourning*—improved consciousness regarding contemporary experiences, awareness of colonial mentality and how it develops;[10] a time when one can lament their victimization.[11]
3. *Dreaming*—improved connection to and pride with the Filipino culture,[12] a time when colonized people can explore their own cultures, experience their own aspirations for the future, and consider their own social order to encompass and express their hopes.[13]
4. *Commitment and Action*—giving back to the community through social action.[14]

What follows is the story of my own decolonization, including some of the things I "discovered" about the Filipino and Filipino American experience along the way.

Approaching Theology

Recovery and Discovery

It wasn't until my late twenties that I found myself in Recovery and Discovery, the phase when a person seeks to deepen their understanding of the history and culture of their people. Through a combination of my graduate school research and moving to an area where I was no longer surrounded by other Filipinos and Filipino Americans, it became obvious just how disconnected I was from my history and all the generations that came before me. When I began reframing my understanding of the Philippines' relationship with Christianity in the wider context of colonization, it was the early descriptions of the islanders that first captured my imagination. The fact that there was an entire way of life that existed long before the Spanish came was a revelation for me, and the act of uncovering the stories of my ancestors was simultaneously a source of pride as well as anger and sadness at how much my ancestors lost.

PRECOLONIAL HISTORY

No written records of precolonial Philippines survived the arrival of the Spanish, who, "in their religious zeal, destroyed the earlier records as completely as possible."[15] Much of what we do know has been gleaned from the records of southeastern Asian countries like India and China, where early settlers of the Philippine islands originated.

From the 700s to the 1400s, the islands were "part of a great Hindu-Malayan empire [that was] ruled from Java and Sumatra in the neighboring islands to the southwest."[16] In the late 1400s, followers of Islam came to the southwestern Sulu Archipelago and Mindanao, where a large Muslim population remains to the present day.

Everything was destroyed, supposedly in the name of Christ. Even at the outset of uncovering my history, it's hard not to give in to the bitterness of only having leftover, borrowed stories and secondhand accounts of what my ancestors were like. What would they have said about themselves, apart from what the world perceived?

When the Spanish arrived in 1521, the islanders they encountered were "culturally diverse groups of indigenous [people]" that were already in the midst of developing a distinct and vibrant culture. Catherine Porter writes, "They had a calendar, weights and measures, a system of writing, some elements of law, some religious ideas showing both Hindu and Mohammedan influences, and had some skill in metalworking, pottery making, and weaving."[17]

Their way of life—my ancestors' way of life—reflected a level of complexity that goes beyond a group of people that were simply trying to survive, beyond the negative and dangerous stereotypes of Filipinos as primitive savages who needed to be civilized. This was news to me, since I'd spent most of my life unquestioningly accepting the idea that anything that happened before the West set foot on the islands wasn't worth knowing.

These early inhabitants of the islands—my ancestors—relied on a deep connection to nature and the land, something that was reflected in their daily life. Homes built in the flatlands were made of materials native to the environment: bamboo, wood, and nipa palm leaves. In the mountains, homes were built on treetops; those living on the coast built their houses on boats or by the shore.

Their livelihoods of farming, fishing, and trading were not just as a means of survival, but areas in which they exhibited skill and expertise. The early Spanish explorers noted my ancestors' skill in "building highly efficient and effective ocean vessels for various purposes such as travel, fishing, war, or trading."[18] More evidence of the genius of the early inhabitants lies in the Banaue rice terraces, which were created in the first century by the Ifugao people in the mountains of north-central Luzon:

> Despite possessing only basic tools, the Ifugao created an engineering marvel: a vast network of rice terraces sustained by an elaborate irrigation system. According to reports, the terraces—which resemble steps carved into the mountainside—cover some 4,000 square miles (10,360 square km), and their total length is estimated at…roughly half the Earth's circumference. While the rice terraces were important to the Ifugao economy, they also served a cultural function, requiring intensive cooperation among the people.[19]

A system of writing, *baybayin*, was likely passed down for generations, using "tree sap as ink and pointed sticks as writing utensils to write on leaves, trees, bamboo tubes and tree barks." This was a surprise to the early Spanish explorers and missionaries who "found out that the majority of the indigenous [people] were literate and proficient in their native alphabet."[20]

How often were the Spanish surprised by the genius of the early islanders? Am I supposed to feel pride, knowing how much my ancestors had accomplished in the generations before 1521? Instead, anger and sadness permeate much of this phase of discovery for me. In getting brief glimpses of what my ancestors were like, I only get a sense of millions of lights being snuffed out because of arrogance and greed spurred on by colonization.

Various forms of art and literature were already present at the time of Spain's arrival in the form of music, dance, and artistic designs of plants, animals, and humans on their pottery and even their tools and weapons. Written and oral literature were passed on among the indigenous peoples about life, celebrating special events and the mundane. Often accompanied by music and dance, there were poems, stories, and songs about

> boating (talindaw), wedding (ihiman), love (kumintang or kundiman), war (kumintang), victor (tagumpay), cradling an infant (hele), fun riddles (bugtong), history (Ifugao Hudhod), and battles of heroic individuals (Indarapatra at Sulayman).[21]

Indigenous mythology, martial arts, spirituality, "all of these were inspired by their natural environments, with mythical creatures being the guardians of mountains, trees, the skies, and oceans who need respect and occasional offerings."[22]

At the time of Spain's arrival, "many indigenous tribes such as the Tagalogs in the region now known as Luzon had evolved a roughly egalitarian social order that was reflected in their mythology; men and women wielded power and held authority in equal measure.[23] A *balangay* or *baranggay* was the "basic unit of government... composed of approximately 60 families...headed by a *Datu* or *Rajah* (Chief), who led in consultation with a council of balangay elders."[24] In this system of government, it was possible for women to "become chiefs in the absence of a male heir" as well as "own property, engage in trade and industry, and often [hold] high positions in society such as a *babaylan*, who were regarded as the healers, shamans, wisdom-keepers, philosophers, and spiritual leaders of a balangay."[25]

Not everything was destroyed. The beauty and art, the traditions, songs, and stories—all of these have endured. And I wonder about the role that I am to play in being a culture bearer, in leaving a legacy for my children and future generations.

AN INHERENTLY RELIGIOUS PEOPLE

In recovering a sense of my history and identity as a Filipino American, learning about the spirituality of my ancestors was particularly significant. According to studies of indigenous religious beliefs and traditions of early Filipinos, there are "three pervading concepts which, since early days, have provided both ground and framework for the early Filipinos' general outlook on life" (numeration is mine):

1. There exists an invisible and powerful spirit world that has contact with and has an effect on the human world. All things in the human world are subject to those in the spirit world.
2. There are spirits everywhere. Objects valued for their supposedly magical powers are believed to be possessed by their respective guardian spirits.
3. All natural events and human activities are always subject to the whims, caprices, and inscrutable ways of the invisible forces in the spirit world. As a result, the spirits must be courted for their favors, or when offended, appeased by appropriate sacrifices and ceremonies...everything needs to be done to ensure that no offense is committed against any spirit.[26]

Based on Spanish accounts of early encounters with the islanders, "Each community had its religious functionaries, usually women, who 'knew' or were familiar with the secrets and normally inscrutable ways of the spirit world."[27] However, there was neither a distinguishable hierarchy nor "established temples for institutionalized worship."[28] T. Valentino Sitoy writes, "Indeed, this lack of temples and a recognizable hierarchy often led the early Spaniards to think mistakenly that the Filipinos did not have any religion at all."[29]

Approaching Theology

Antonio Pigafetta, a member and archivist of Magellan's expedition, provides "the earliest European eyewitness account of a traditional Filipino sacrifice."[30] He describes "in detail a traditional religious sacrifice (*pagdiwata*) performed by two very old priestesses."[31] In it, they invoke the deities and spirits with instruments and dance by offering up dishes of food. A blood sacrifice is then offered, in the form of a hog, and its blood is smeared onto the foreheads of those present. The ceremony concludes with the priestesses, and all the women present, eating the dishes of food.[32] Religious worship among the islanders followed this same general structure (i.e., an invocation to the deities and spirits, a blood sacrifice, and then offerings of food, a betel-nut mixture).[33] Interestingly enough, "from the various accounts available, there is little doubt that pre-Islamic or pre-Christian Philippine religion, at least structurally, was quite the same throughout the various islands of the archipelago."[34]

As described in *A History of Christianity in Asia, Africa, and Latin America*, the first missionaries to the Philippines typically "interpreted the religion of the people as all the work of the devil, whose influence and presence they felt tangibly."[35] These early missionaries demonized the local worship practices:

> All their method of government and their religion is based on tradition and custom introduced by the devil himself, who used to speak to them in their idols and their ministers. They preserved these traditions in songs which they know by memory, having learned them as children by hearing them sung when rowing, when working, when rejoicing and celebrating, and much more when weeping in mourning for the dead. In these barbaric songs they tell of the fabled genealogies and vain deeds of their gods.[36]

But what if we read between the lines? Without the filter of suspicion and fear, I see a self-governing people with a faith system rooted in tradition and custom. I see a people that felt deeply, that loved their children, that sang when they were happy and sang even more when they were sad. I see a people of insurmountable faith, storytellers with boundless imaginations. I see myself in these people that lived generations ago, and claim the stories and dreams of my ancestors that continue to live on through and within me.

God of My Ancestors

In the eyes of the missionaries, the unfamiliar customs of the Filipinos were, without question, replete with idol worship and mass deception:

> Among them they make one a principal one and superior to all. This one the Tagalogs call *Bathala Mei-capal*, that is to say, the god who is Maker or Creator, and the Visayans, *Laon*, which means Antiquity. They speak of the creation of the world, the beginning of the human race, the flood, the reward of glory, punishment and other invisible things. Doing this they tell innumerable falsehoods and even vary a great deal in telling them, some doing it in one fashion, others in another. Thus it can best be seen that they are lies and fables....To sum it up, their idolatry like that of many other nations, consists in adoring and considering as gods their ancestors, particularly men who were outstanding for their deeds of valor or cruelty. In memory of their ancestors they have little idols, some of stone, others of straw, others of bone or ivory or of a crocodile's tooth, others of gold, which they call *Iarawan*, which means idol, image, or statue. To these they had recourse in their necessities and offered to them their barbaric sacrifices.[37]

But what if we look for the Spirit and rummage through the pages of these stories? What if we find God hiding in plain sight? In the hearts of these people who were trying to make sense of their world, much as we do now? What if Bathala Mei-capal or Laon are just different names of the same God revealed to Abraham, Isaac, and Jacob? That the stories of creation, of the flood are facets of the same gem that we turn over and over in quiet contemplation? What if the ancestors that they honored were of the same community of saints named in the New Testament, bearing witness to the ongoing work of the Spirit who knows no boundaries?

When encountering the indigenous spiritual leaders, Spanish missionaries came across "a tradition of *babaylanes* or priestesses: women (or feminized men) serving as gateways and intercessors to the divine in matters of sacred ritual."[38] All of them, men and women alike, were interpreted as "practitioners of trickery and devil worship":

Approaching Theology

> Although they did not have any temples, they had priests, men and women, whom the Tagalogs call *Catalonan* and the Visayans *Babailan*. This office was held by the one who had the best ability to deal with the devil, who deceived him, or with the blind people, to deceive them with a thousand tricks and deceptions.[39]

What would the islands be like if women and men had continued to lead and wield power in equal measure? What would our worship look like if all God's people were able to bring their gifts to the altar? If the nuances and strengths and personalities of the entire spectrum of humanity were invited to be gateways to the divine? How would it be different? What would the world look like?

THE ARRIVAL OF THE WEST

It was March 1521—Easter Sunday, the accounts say—when a Spanish expedition led by Portuguese explorer Ferdinand Magellan arrived on the shores of the archipelago now known as the Philippines. Apparently the Christian faith was introduced to the islands (Cebu, more precisely), with a literal bang:

> About fifty soldiers in their best clothes, without body armor but carrying their weapons, came onshore for the Mass (the first in the Philippines)....As soon as the boats reached the shore, six guns from the fleet were discharged, "as a sign of peace"....At the elevation of the Sacred Host, all the fleet's artillery were fired in one salvo, at a signal of muskets from shore. After Mass, Magellan arranged a fencing tournament to further impress the local people with Spanish might. As a parting gesture afterwards, the Spanish troops once more formed in order, and fired all their muskets.[40]

From the very beginning, "whether by accident or by design, Spanish military might have played a prominent role in these ceremonies."[41] Promises of safety and protection from both human and supernatural forces were made to the islanders, conditional on the placement of "a large cross on a prominent spot on the island."[42] They were told,

Whenever other Spanish ships would come in the future, they would know that some of their fellows had been there earlier and would therefore do nothing to harm the Limasawa islanders nor damage their property....If anyone among them should in the future be captured by the Europeans, they would immediately be released upon showing the sign of the cross.[43]

With regard to the supernatural, Magellan promised that "should the islanders adore the cross upon seeing it every morning, 'neither thunder, lightning nor storms would harm them in the least.'" And so it was that

the impression that Kolambu's people received of the efficacy of the crossed-wood religious symbol was that it not only had the supernatural power to protect one from natural calamities; it was also a useful sign to use in winning the friendship of any other white-skinned visitors from beyond the seas.[44]

A few thousands of Cebuano islanders were baptized in 1521, the declarations of Magellan likely striking a chord with them, who promised

he would regard and treat better those who became Christians like the Europeans. He also promised to present the Cebuanos with a suit of armor once they were baptized. He likewise assured them that the demon they feared would no longer appear to them till the hour of their death.[45]

Sitoy writes, "The healing powers attributed to baptism and the belief that Christian ceremonials and symbols were effective against the dreaded evil spirits drew masses of Filipinos to the new faith."[46]

All things considered, it would stand to reason that the chief of Cebu, Rajah Humabon, along with the rest of the natives, "apparently primarily understood their baptism as a ceremonial act of sealing peace and forging an alliance with the European visitors."[47] Consequently, "it did not seem to have occurred to them that their new status as 'baptized Christians' implied a religious quality that would stand in judgment on their continued practice of heathen religious rites."[48] These factors, in addition to the observation that from the very beginning, Filipinos have "always been an inherently religious people"[49] (based on the central role that religion played in various anti-Spanish revolts), all contributed to the significant number of conversions to Christianity that took place in the Philippines in the years of Spanish colonial rule.

There was a brief period from 1521 to 1565, between the arrival of Magellan's expedition and the colonization of Spain (or, as Sitoy phrases it, when "the first permanent conversions"[50] of the islanders took place). The sources that I initially used to study the Catholic Church's history in the Philippines conveniently gloss over this brief but important interlude. Magellan, you see, was killed by a poison arrow in April 1521 in the Battle of Mactan. Not all the archipelago's indigenous inhabitants were willing to cooperate or submit to Spain's conquest of the islands. A group of native warriors, led by the Mactan chief Lapu Lapu, who "denied the overlordship of Humabon or the king of Spain,"[51] was successful in defending the island of Mactan. This resistance subsequently gave over forty years of freedom to the islands before Spain's return in 1565.

With the arrival of more religious orders in the years following 1565 came a more systematic and dehumanizing approach to catechizing the natives. In 1579, Franciscan Juan de Plasencia introduced the "Philippine reductions," a course of action that was meant to "facilitate the evangelization of the Filipino natives"[52] in the face of a growing number of converts and a shortage of religious missionaries. According to Ordanico De La Pena, the Philippine reductions involved the suppression of smaller villages so that towns and cities could be formed. He writes, "Some of the Filipino natives were forced to abandon the forests and highlands in order to settle in the lowlands and coastal areas";[53] they were "organized and ordered to settle and to live in one location."[54]

The *encomienda* system was also introduced by the Spanish government, and was a response to the question of who would govern the natives. In this system, "Local lands were ceded to Spanish colonies, giving them the right to demand labor from the natives in exchange for protection and religious instruction."[55] In 1597, the Filipino natives living in a town under the *encomienda* system went to a church building every Sunday and holy days for the Eucharistic Mass and religious instruction. This Eucharistic Mass was preceded by devotional prayers and the Catechism....The natives were advised and encouraged to attend church service as often as possible....The Catechism was recited before the Mass in the church, while the natives started to enter the church. A priest or one of the elders led the reading in a loud voice, and the rest of the people in the church repeated what was being read.[56]

By 1620, "nearly half the Filipinos subject to Spanish rule had been converted, though mostly nominally."[57] Sitoy writes, "in the next 275 years or so of Spanish rule, the other half was converted." By the year 1700, "all coastal and lowland Filipinos (except in those southern territories under the strong sway of Islam) had been baptized."[58]

In the more recent past, Spanish Governor-General Narciso Claveria y Zaldua issued a decree in 1849 requiring the use of surnames by all residents of the Philippines. Those who did not have family surnames were issued one of the names written in *The Catalogo Alfabetico de Apellidos*, which "contains 141 pages of surnames with both Spanish and indigenous roots."[59] Anri Ichimura writes, "The catalog explains that, in 1849, the provincial governors simply allocated each town several pages from the catalog, from which the townspeople chose their surnames. The result: To this day, there are many families in provincial towns that share the same first letter in their surname."[60]

> "For example, in the Bikol region, the entire alphabet is laid out like a garland over the provinces of Albay, Sorsogon, and Catanduanes, which in 1849, belonged to the jurisdiction of Albay," the catalog states.
>
> "Beginning with A at the provincial capital, the letters B and C mark the towns along the coast beyond Tabaco and Tiwi. We return and trace along the coast of Sorsogon the letters E to L; then starting down the Iraya Valley at Daraga with M, we stop with S to Polangui and Libon, and finish the alphabet with a quick tour around the island of Catanduanes."[61]

Approaching Theology

Mourning

In the decolonization phase of Mourning, a person begins connecting their current experiences with the historical experiences of their people, when one becomes aware of colonial mentality.[62] It is a time "when one is able to lament their victimization."[63]

As I take this time to remember the story of my ancestors, it becomes increasingly difficult to unsee the damage that was wrought by the Catholic Church in the name of the missions and claiming the land for Christ. In the guise of spreading the gospel and civilizing the islanders, the church was complicit in stripping away the peoples' identities and land. I imagine the deep pain and grief of my ancestors, whose songs of mourning over all that was lost reverberate throughout generations of their descendants. Over time, the recognition that my life—my present joy and suffering—is somehow intertwined with the joy and suffering of my ancestors is a thread that helps me reconnect to my past and recover a sense of my identity I hadn't realized was missing. This act of remembering moves me further along the journey of coming home to myself.

The Filipino national hero José Rizal (1861–96), in describing the Filipino condition under Spanish rule, encapsulates the deep loss of identity that happened as a result of colonization:

> Little by little they lost their old traditions, the mementos of their past; they gave up their writing, their songs, their poems, their laws in order to learn by rote other doctrines which they did not understand, another morality, another aesthetics different from those inspired by their climate and their manner of thinking. Then they declined, degrading themselves in their own eyes; they became ashamed of what was their own; they began to admire and praise whatever was foreign and incomprehensible; their spirit was dismayed and it surrendered.
>
> Thus passed away years and centuries. Religious pomp, the rituals, songs, lights, images dressed in gold that appealed to the eyes, the cult in a mysterious language, the stories, the miracles, and the sermons hypnotized the spirit of the people, by nature already superstitious, though

without succeeding to destroy it completely, despite the system that was followed with implacable tenacity.[64]

For the past several years, it has become more obvious to me that much of my growing unease with the faith tradition I inherited is because I am in mourning. Mourning for my ancestors. Letting go of who I once was—the person that understood the world in binary terms: black and white, good and evil, wrong and right. Any version of myself that ever felt *sure* of anything is slowly fading from memory. As I piece together the long-forgotten memories of my ancestors, in the aftermath of the contentious 2016 election, in the midst of navigating a global pandemic—all the expectations I used to have about how people of faith were supposed to care for their neighbors, how we were supposed to welcome the stranger, how we were supposed to *listen* to each other...none of it turned out the way I thought it would.

Dreaming

In the decolonization phase of Dreaming, a person connects more deeply to their culture with pride.[65] It is "a time when colonized people are able to explore their own cultures, experience their own aspirations for the future, and consider their own social order to encompass and express their hopes."[66] I experience this phase fleetingly, but am aware that this desire to dream is present, even if just as a small seed. For now, my dreaming mostly comes in the form of questions and wonder: How then do I make sense, make meaning of all of this? What are the implications of holding on to a faith tradition that was complicit in the oppression of my ancestors? How do I understand my own identity and inherent dignity? How do I reconcile the cognitive dissonance?

I look again, rummaging through the pages of the past, and I look for Christ where he always is: in the margins. With the poor and the oppressed, with the powerless and the disenfranchised. With the lost and the forgotten. And I see Christ singing in mourning with my ancestors, weeping over the loss of beauty, creativity, and life.

I look again, naming the injustices committed by the Catholic Church and its representatives, rejecting the acts of subjugation and oppression, standing in solidarity with all who have suffered because of greed and the lust for power.

I look again, remembering the stories told by my ancestors and hear the whispers of the Spirit and see Christ's fingerprints, "for in him all things in heaven and on earth were created, things visible and invisible, whether thrones or dominions or rulers or powers—all things have been created through him and for him" (Col 1:16).

There is a description of Filipino spirituality by Fred Cordova that has always resonated with me, in which he calls it

> the ultimate flowering of "Indo-Malayan spirituality in the complexities of Catholicism." Despite forced conversion by the Spanish, Filipinos preserved an "innate sense of spirituality" that has made church life central to the Filipino American experience.[67]

In many ways, this recognition that Catholicism found fertile ground in the islands because "Christianity in its Catholic form was congenial with traditional Filipino animistic religion"[68] and that "the structure and worldview of pre-Christian Filipino religion dovetailed with those of Catholicism"[69] helps me strengthen the connection with my ancestors. It is a reminder that the faith that I have now is rooted in a heritage that existed long before 1521.

I think also of Peter Phan's words about popular devotion in light of the "postmodern and postcolonial understanding of culture."[70] In this postcolonial understanding, culture is not simply "a sharply demarcated, self-contained, homogeneous, and integrated whole,"[71] but "a ground of contest in relations and as a historically evolving, fragmented, inconsistent, conflicted, constructed, ever-shifting, and porous social reality."[72] He writes,

> In this contest of relations the role of power in the shaping of cultural identity is of paramount importance, a factor that the modern concept of culture largely ignores. In the past, anthropologists tended to regard culture as an innocent set of conventions rather than a reality of conflict in which the colonizers, the powerful, the wealthy, the victors, the dominant can obliterate the beliefs and values of the colonized, the weak, the poor, the vanquished, the

subjugated, so that there has been, in Serge Gruzinski's expression, "la colonization de l'imaginaire." This role of power, as Michel Foucault and other masters of suspicion have argued, is central in the formation of knowledge in general. In the formation of cultural identity the role of power is even more extensive, since it is constituted by groups of people with conflicting interests, and the winners can dictate their cultural terms to the losers.[73]

In light of this postmodern and postcolonial understanding of culture, Phan observes that "it is easy to appreciate popular devotion as a form of resistance and subversion, as well as compromise and appropriation of the official religion."[74] He mentions ways in which others in the field of theology have come to this same appreciation:

> Keith Pecklers, in the wake of Latin American theologians, highlights the ways in which popular devotion has opened up alternative access to the divine, especially in the Marian devotion and different forms of blessing, and has privileged the role of women as domestic priestesses.[75]

According to Ofelia Villero, "the animistic belief system of the indigenes did not disappear, but was grafted onto Catholic rituals and devotional practices to form the foundation of Filipino popular religiosity."[76] She writes,

> Filipino Catholicism is characterized by an emphasis on pietistic behavior—primarily innumerable devotional practices, novenas, processions, and pilgrimages—rather than doctrinal and moral preoccupations. The pattern is followed by numerous Filipino Americans who have introduced to the United States numerous Filipino Catholic devotions and celebrations like the devotion to Our Lady of Peace and Good Voyage (also called the Virgin of Antipolo, named after a town in the province of Rizal) and the Santo Niño (Holy Child) festival.[77]

I smile to myself, wondering what my grandma would have thought of me calling her nightly devotion "resistance rosaries." I think of all the subversive *lolas* and aunties leading prayer meetings and novenas, how it was a given that I was expected to lead and teach. I think of the exuberant music and joyful singing and dancing that come so naturally to the Filipinos and Filipino Americans I was surrounded by at church. I think of how so much of what I know about Filipino culture, I know because of other Filipino Catholics. And I see the Spirit breaking through, bringing forth the threads of my ancestors, weaving a beautiful tapestry of joy and sorrow, pain, and beauty. And here I find Christ sitting with me, waiting for whatever comes next.

NOTES

1. Poka Laenui, "Processes of Decolonization," in *Reclaiming Indigenous Voice and Vision*, ed. Marie Battiste (Vancouver: UBC Press, 2000), 150.
2. Eric John Ramos David, *Brown Skin, White Minds: Filipino-/American Postcolonial Psychology*, with commentaries (Charlotte, NC: Information Age Publishing, 2013), 19.
3. David, *Brown Skin, White Minds*, 63.
4. David, *Brown Skin, White Minds*, 63.
5. David, *Brown Skin, White Minds*, 65.
6. David, *Brown Skin, White Minds*, 65.
7. Laenui, "Processes of Decolonization," 152–59.
8. See David, *Brown Skin, White Minds*, 180.
9. David, *Brown Skin, White Minds*, 180.
10. David, *Brown Skin, White Minds*, 180.
11. Laenui, "Processes of Decolonization," 154.
12. David, *Brown Skin, White Minds*, 180.
13. Laenui, "Processes of Decolonization," 155.
14. David, *Brown Skin, White Minds*, 180.
15. Catherine Porter, *EM 24: What Lies Ahead for the Philippines?* (Washington, DC: United States War Department, 1945), https://www.historians.org/about-aha-and-membership/aha-history-and-archives/gi-roundtable-series/pamphlets/em-24-what-lies-ahead-for-the-philippines-(1945)/when-did-philippine-history-begin.
16. Porter, *What Lies Ahead?*
17. Porter, *What Lies Ahead?*

18. David, *Brown Skin, White Minds*, 8.
19. Amy Tikkanen, "Banaue Rice Terraces," *Encyclopedia Britannica*, https://www.britannica.com/place/Banaue-rice-terraces.
20. David, *Brown Skin, White Minds*, 8.
21. David, *Brown Skin, White Minds*, 6.
22. David, *Brown Skin, White Minds*, 7.
23. Rachel Bundang, "May You Storm Heaven with Your Prayers: Devotions to Mary and Jesus in Filipino American Catholic Life," in *Off the Menu: Asian and Asian North American Women's Religion and Theology*, ed. Rita Nakashima Brock, Jung Ha Kim, and Kwok Pui-Lan (Louisville, KY: Westminster John Knox Press, 2007), 93.
24. David, *Brown Skin, White Minds*, 10.
25. David, *Brown Skin, White Minds*, 10.
26. T. Valentino Sitoy Jr., *A History of Christianity in the Philippines* (Quezon City, Philippines: Cellar Book Shop, 1985), 1–2.
27. Sitoy, *History of Christianity in the Philippines*, 18.
28. Sitoy, *History of Christianity in the Philippines*, 18.
29. Sitoy, *History of Christianity in the Philippines*, 18.
30. Sitoy, *History of Christianity in the Philippines*, 20.
31. Sitoy, *History of Christianity in the Philippines*, 51.
32. Sitoy, *History of Christianity in the Philippines*, 51–52.
33. Sitoy, *History of Christianity in the Philippines*, 19.
34. Sitoy, *History of Christianity in the Philippines*, 22.
35. Klaus Koschorke, Frider Ludwig, Mariano Delgado, and Roland Spliesgart, eds., *A History of Christianity in Asia, Africa, and Latin America, 1450–1990* (Grand Rapids, MI: Eerdmans, 2007), 22.
36. Koschorke et al., *History of Christianity in Asia, Africa, and Latin America*, 22.
37. Koschorke et al., *History of Christianity in Asia, Africa, and Latin America*, 22.
38. Bundang, "May You Storm Heaven with Your Prayers," 93.
39. Koschorke et al., *History of Christianity in Asia, Africa, and Latin America*, 22.
40. Sitoy, *History of Christianity*, 40.
41. Sitoy, *History of Christianity*, 40.
42. Sitoy, *History of Christianity*, 40–41.
43. Sitoy, *History of Christianity*, 40–41.
44. Sitoy, *History of Christianity*, 40–41.
45. Sitoy, *History of Christianity*, 45–46.

46. T. Valentino Sitoy Jr., "Philippines," in *A Dictionary of Asian Christianity*, ed. Scott W. Sunquist (Grand Rapids, MI: Eerdmans, 2001), 655.

47. Sitoy, *History of Christianity*, 51.

48. Sitoy, *History of Christianity*, 51.

49. Sitoy, "Philippines," *Dictionary of Asian Christianity*, 655.

50. Sitoy, "Philippines," *Dictionary of Asian Christianity*, 655.

51. Jose Amiel Angeles, "The Battle of Mactan and the Indigenous Discourse on War," *Philippine Studies* 55, no. 1 (2007): 3–52.

52. Ordanico De la Pena, *The Birth of the Catholic Philippines in Asia: Includes the Lives of San Lorenzo Ruiz and Blessed Pedro Calungsod* (n.p.: Xlibris, 2001), 22.

53. De la Pena, *Birth of the Catholic Philippines in Asia*, 22.

54. De la Pena, *Birth of the Catholic Philippines in Asia*, 44.

55. De la Pena, *Birth of the Catholic Philippines in Asia*, 46.

56. De la Pena, *Birth of the Catholic Philippines in Asia*, 47.

57. Sitoy, "Philippines," 655.

58. Sitoy. "Philippines," 655.

59. Anri Ichimura, "Find Your Family Name in This Catalog of Historical Surnames from the Spanish Colonial Era," *Esquire Philippines*, November 2, 2019, https://www.esquiremag.ph/culture/books-and-art/surname-spanish-catalog-a00304-20191102.

60. Ichimura, "Find Your Family Name."

61. Ichimura, "Find Your Family Name."

62. David, *Brown Skin, White Minds*, 180.

63. Laenui, "Processes of Decolonization," 154.

64. Filipinas E. Pineda, Diosdado G. Capino, and Maria Minerva A. Gonzelez, *Rizal's Life, Works, and Writings: Their Impact on Our National Identity* (Philippines: JMC Press, 1977), 220.

65. David, *Brown Skin, White Minds*, 180.

66. Laenui, "Processes of Decolonization," 155.

67. Fred Cordova, *Filipinos: Forgotten Asian Americans* (Dubuque, IA: Kendall/Hunt, 1983), as quoted in Lance D. Laird, "Religions of the Pacific Rim in the Pacific Northwest," in *Religion and Public Life in the Pacific Northwest: The None Zone*, ed. Patricia O'Connell Killen and Mark Silk (Lanham, MD: AltaMira Press, 2004), 116.

68. Sitoy, "Philippines," 655.

69. Sitoy, "Philippines," 655.

70. Peter Phan, *In Our Own Tongues* (Maryknoll, NY: Orbis Books, 2003), 88.
71. Phan, *In Our Own Tongues*, 88.
72. Phan, *In Our Own Tongues*, 88.
73. Phan, *In Our Own Tongues*, 66–67.
74. Phan, *In Our Own Tongues*, 88.
75. Phan, *In Our Own Tongues*, 88.
76. Ofelia O. Villero, "Filipino Americans: Religion," in *Encyclopedia of Asian American Folklore and Folklife*, vol. 1, ed. Jonathan H. X. Lee and Kathleen M. Nadeau (Santa Barbara, CA: ABC-CLIO, 2010), 403.
77. Villero, "Filipino Americans: Religion," 401.

PART 2
PRACTICING THEOLOGY

7

FOR WHOM ARE WE OUTRAGED?

Maria Gwyn McDowell

The Sunday after photos were released of children caged in migrant facilities along our southern border, I did not preach about tearing children from the arms of their parents.[1] I did not, as a longtime friend insisted his clergy do, address the evil being done on our behalf at the border. What I did was pray. During the Prayers of the People, a time we leave open for anyone to speak their heart to God, I asked for forgiveness for a nation that has torn children from their parents for the entirety of our history, a nation for whom such violence is in our DNA, a nation whose survival has rested on inflicting terror on those whose very presence is perceived as a threat to our way of life. And I prayed that we would become a people who resist such violence. I know that prayer is, by many, seen as a passive response in a time that needs action. Frankly, I tend to agree, if by prayer we assume that we can rightfully separate word from action. A prayer on which we do not act is no prayer at all; it is a platitude, a comfort to the afflicters, and affliction to the afflicted.

The context of my ministry, however, requires a different emphasis. Every Sunday I stand as a white priest amid a congregation founded by the descendants of women and men enslaved by colonial powers in the Caribbean and North America. A congregation whose members helped found the Portland Chapters of the NAACP and the Urban League. A congregation composed of people who were doctors, dentists, lawyers, and civil rights activists in the only state welcomed into the union as a whites-only homeland. It makes no sense to use my sermons to parse the biblical prooftexting of Attorney General Jeff Sessions, who like so many before him used Romans 13 to demand obedience to unjust state authority, in front of a people who could not legally own property in my home state until 1952. It makes no sense to do so in front of those whose bodies have experienced the profound, and entirely legal, injustice of a state that allowed the separation of Black children from Black, legally enslaved, parents whose bodies were regarded, in the blunt words of Kelly Brown Douglas, as perpetually guilty chattel.[2] No one who has studied history in light of justice and compassion should be under any illusion that "law" and "justice" are always or even necessarily the same thing, a reality my parish lives every day. I no longer have (if I ever really did) the luxury of shocked liberal outrage over the choice of the U.S. government to interpret our laws in such a way that terrorizes families, because this state-sponsored terror is simply the long, historical reality of the people among whom I preach every Sunday.

The Virtue of Anger

Truthfully, I was outraged at such deliberately destructive interpretations of our laws, which, it is worth repeating, were not created by Donald Trump, but by supposedly immigrant-friendly Democratic legislators and executors. I was angry, and anger is an emotion that over the years has served me well. It was anger at a religious tradition I loved that would not let me remain content with the sexist practices of my church, and that anger gave me the energy to persist in offering alternative theological interpretations. However, much of the anger I was witnessing in my social media feeds fell into what a friend called "recreational anger."[3] "Recreational anger" is that performative anger that lets everyone know we are on the right side of an issue, that we are "woke" and "get it," but that neither discerns nor requires action. It is the kind of anger that rarely demands that we listen and learn how we might be complicit in the very actions that support the structures against which we rail in media posts filled with

For Whom Are We Outraged?

wit, snark, and flags-with-all-the-right-color-stripes. Recreational anger does not require us to change our behavior as individuals, and more importantly—since too often we reduce change to individual action—it does not motivate us to the kind of community organizations required to address the structures created to cement injustice: police organizations created to protect the business and propertied classes; police unions that protect the right of officers to kill over the rights of Blacks to live; religious organizations who deny women reproductive justice; corporations who are accountable to shareholders but not the flourishing of their workers, to name only a few. Too often, this kind of recreational anger not only lets many of us off the hook of difficult action, but also confirms our worst fears about anger itself.

At a fundamental and intuitive level, anger is an emotional response to recognizing diminished dignity or conditions that prevent the flourishing of either an individual or a group. Anger is understandable, but it is very often dismissed as dangerous due to the assumption that anger and aggression go hand in hand. Anger, it is assumed, only ever results in retribution. Michael Jaycox is a white Christian ethicist who examines the role of emotions in public life, with a focus on racial justice and the work of theologians and ethicists of color. The fear we have regarding anger, he says, is that anger "actually subverts justice while intending to advance justice."[4] What better illustrates this than the white supremacist fear that Black and brown power will result in white demise? This fear underscores the fundamental white belief that white "justice" is envisioned as punishment and retribution rather than restoration. This assumption about the nature of justice makes entirely reasonable the fear that if the "other" holds power, it will be used to exact violent retribution.

But this fear is not held only by avowed white supremacists. So deep is the white fear that anger and retribution are inevitably paired that thinkers such as Martha Nussbaum, who once saw the benefits of anger as a protective force for human flourishing, now reject it as unavoidably destructive.[5] Jaycox draws attention to the timing of her switch in light of the Black Lives Matter movement, and interprets it as a move protective of the very same white, liberal establishment that structurally preserves an eschatological vision of constant progress through implementation of "fair," "reasonable," and consistent processes. Yet there is mounting evidence that "good" process does not create justice for all but only stability for the white powerbrokers that control the process. Our traditional democratic processes are themselves deeply, and racially, exclusive.[6]

The assumption of anger as inherently destructive silences the voices of those who dare to question the status quo in a manner that is not full of gentle humor, dignified comportment, and reasoned conversation. Examples abound. In response to an essay that opened a discussion of homosexual intercourse with a "thought experiment" involving fat pills and sexbots, I offered a sarcastically substantive response. This response was rejected for publication on the same forum as the original post, not because I did not have valid points (an editor affirmed the substance of my criticisms), but because my response lacked civility.[7] Male-defined civility was more important than substantive criticism. Yet anger at the repeated spread of lies (in this case, that same-sex intercourse is always depersonalized), anger at the refusal to listen to the voices of those who are wronged, or anger at the utter denial of history in order to preserve the illusions of one's present, are entirely normal, reasonable, and justified. Think here of the anger voiced by #MeToo, a movement started by a Black woman, ignored, adopted by a swath of primarily white women, and repeatedly dismissed by men and their supportive media as irrational. Rebecca Traister notes that "women have been told to behave when they are angry: to not let anyone know, and to joke and to be sweet and rational and vulnerable."[8] Christy Blaise Ford "spoke carefully, precisely, in a high voice; she made jokes about caffeine, asked deferentially about whether it would be O.K. to take a break." But the man whom she accused of sexual assault, "Brett Kavanaugh bellowed; he snarled; he pouted and wept furiously at the injustice of having his ascendance to power interrupted by accusations of sexual assault."[9] Men are allowed to marshal fury, but women are routinely denied that form of expression and denigrated when they break the rules.

Returning to the racialization of anger, Jaycox, following Charles Mills, notes that the white liberal project requires the absence of anger at oppression precisely to keep white supremacy invisible. White supremacy must remain invisible to ensure that whites bear no guilt for their participation, and thus do not earn retribution. He highlights Audre Lorde, James Baldwin, and James Cone as rightly angry authors whose voices must be listened to, an imperative consistent with his and my convictions that liberative theologies must arise from the voices of those who have experienced oppression. What their "normatively realized social anger" does is offer a "cognitive interruption of the ideological rationalizations for privilege and oppression."[10] This interruption is required to launch all of us out of the inertia that too often grips us in the face of the overwhelming persistence of injustice.

Jaycox focuses on the social aspect of anger as a cognitive interruption of the normality of injustice. "Social anger," defines Jaycox, "is a transgressive judgment that systemic injustice is stymieing the basic human flourishing of a vulnerable social group."[11] It is when witnesses to injustice "finally give themselves permission to think more critically about the racism, sexism, and classism they had previously accepted as 'normal.'"[12] Note that Jaycox is speaking of *social* anger, of *social groups*. Too often, we reduce sin and repentance to individual acts of vice or virtue, ironically referring to such acts as a form of social consciousness: recycling, driving less, talking to the racist uncle, welcoming your gay children. Such acts are indeed conscious of the social nature of our individual lives, but they are not necessarily social action for significant social change. Much of the injustice of the world is not the result of individual sin but is social and structural in nature. White supremacy is not (only) the problem of individuals, but of lending systems that devalued entire neighborhoods if a single Black family moved in, banks that denied home repair loans to Blacks, the refusal to provide reproductive justice to women of many shades, and the moral and legal acceptability of standing your ground with violence—domestic or gun-wielding. These are systematic, structural problems, and require a systematic and structural change that can only be implemented by social *groups*, not just individuals.[13]

Outrage or "recreational anger" is simply not enough in the face of the kinds of injustice which thrive in our world. Outrage too easily tends to serve only our own performative needs to appear virtuous. What we need is an anger rooted in truthful history, responsibility toward the other, and commitment to restorative justice.

Responsible Anger

I was gratified after church on the same Sunday that I did not preach my outrage to open my social media to a stream of reminders that the United States was founded on practices that separated Black, Native American, and Japanese children from their parents. I was grateful to read Katie Grimes's reminder that we regularly violate the parent-child bond of the incarcerated, that we are entirely too willing to view those children as unworthy of our compassion.[14] We do this, we have done this, in the name of "safety and prosperity," polite terms that mask the imperialistic conviction that it remains the Manifest Destiny of whites to own and control this land as if it is, and always has been, our land. Truthfully understanding history is an essential first step toward social change. Visceral objection to truthful history, such as the suppression of anything that smacks of Critical Race Theory, highlights the ways that illusions of the past preserve the beneficial structures of the present. History is an essential start, but it is not enough. Men can read books about sexism and well-intentioned whites can read about Black and brown experiences (I know many who do) without committing to an essential next step: taking responsibility for the present.

Much of the outrage over caged children at the border failed to ask a crucial question: Who is responsible for those who are here? Catholic ethicist Tisha Rajendra frames justice as "responsibility to relationships," and repeatedly points out that the stories we tell about immigrants relieve us, the receiving nation, of real responsibility.[15] We characterize immigrants as fleeing desperate poverty (though in reality the desperately poor generally lack the resources to emigrate) and so can blame their plight on the fiscal irresponsibility of their home nation. Or, their nation is dangerous and corrupt, conveniently ignoring that perhaps our drug addiction might be exacerbating the problem. The United States is the benevolent nation that can choose to accept or reject immigrants. But we have no responsibility for any of them.

Yet Rajendra's argument is not that we have responsibility for all immigrants everywhere, but for particular immigrants here. We are responsible for those that arrive at *our* borders. Why? Because they arrive at *our borders in particular* due to already existing relationships: the *Bracero* program; the historical family connections between citizens of what is currently Mexico and the United States that go back to a time when much of what is now the United States was actually Mexico; trade policies that create language and economic dependency through foreign investment. This list can go on.

For Whom Are We Outraged?

Every Sunday when I preach, responsibility quells my outrage. Outrage may be an important first step, but when it fails to ask the right questions, questions rooted in our relationships with one another, it is a noisy gong and a clanging cymbal (1 Cor 13:1). What responsibilities flow from the relationship already existing in this place? What does it mean to be in a parish founded in 1911 because the Black members of the (then) Cathedral of the Diocese of (now Western) Oregon were a source of "discomfort" and were courteously invited to leave and form their own "colored mission"? What does it mean to be responsible as a white priest in a historically Black parish? What does it mean to be an increasingly diverse (that is, less Black) parish in a historically Black but now rapidly gentrifying (meaning, whiter) neighborhood?

Historically Conscious Anger

MT Dávila highlights the centrality of historical consciousness in the work of Kelly Brown Douglas, Patrick Cheng, Jennifer Harvey, and Vincent Lloyd, all Christian ethicists wrestling with racial justice.[16] Every author she discusses *begins* by telling the historical reality of the founding and building of white America: the settling of stolen land through the labor of cheap(er) subjugated labor, justified by a Christian ideology that emphasizes the dark side of the exodus story, not as a story of freedom from slavery, but a violent possessing of a previously occupied land and the genocide of its inhabitants. Their purpose is, says Dávila, to

> raise difficult questions, not just about particular incidents in U.S. history where Christian churches promoted racist ideologies and failed to decry massive racial oppression, but about the ways these ideas and failures embedded themselves in the growing consensus on the common good, the attitude of the nation-state toward marginalized communities, notions of political and social equality, cultural rights, law and criminal justice, and the civic order in general.[17]

It was fellow *WIT* member Amaryah Shaye Jones-Armstrong who drew my attention to Jennifer Harvey in particular. Jones-Armstrong expressed concern that Christian "reconciliation" language assumes that all parties *want* to be in relationship, to be reconciled. This remains a colonialist assumption, where power is utilized to force unwanted relationship. Harvey identifies this inherent imbalance in white Christian efforts to reconcile, drawing attention to the *difference* between white and nonwhite communities, which, when understood, properly puts the burden on white communities to first come to terms with whiteness. The moral burden is quite different for white and communities of color, and that must be recognized before any relationship is offered. Harvey argues that continued segregation at the eleven o'clock hour on a Sunday morning signifies the need for a paradigm of reparations.[18] Harvey bases her analysis on James Cone's argument that white talk of the "beloved community" fails to take seriously what we must do to get there. Reparations are fundamentally about repairing relationships damaged by a particular party. Reconciliation is simply not possible without first repairing what was, and remains, broken. In our conversation, Jones-Armstrong suggested that rather than insisting on relationship, we might also need to consider a sort of "ethical indifference, such that our lives could take the shape they take without having to be in coerced relation to others but also acknowledging the social obligations we have to each other as something that is not an infringement on our freedom."[19] It is entirely reasonable that one party in a relationship might simply not want to be in a relationship, except for the ways in which proximity (physical, situational) creates obligations. Here the responsibility created by voluntary and involuntary relationships noted by Rajendra, rooted in accurate historical consciousness and an awareness of difference, must also account for the way in which one party might, or might not, want to be in relationship.

The Pace of Social Change

One of the failures of easy expressions of outrage is that too often, it fails to move us, or provides an excuse to avoid essential next steps. Anger, in particular what Jaycox calls "social anger," can provide the fuel for significant social change. Rosa Parks was no stranger to anger and resistance. But the ten-year-old Rosa Parks swinging a brick at a would-be rapist has a different kind of anger than the

For Whom Are We Outraged?

woman who in her later years steadfastly kept her seat, a decision strategically planned and supported by a community who channeled their rage into creative, decisive, provocative action meant to publicly highlight and shame injustice.[20] Anger in isolation is not enough. Strategic action takes the support of a community; it takes time, and often repetition. Pauli Murray organized lunch counter sit-ins while a law student at Howard University, in 1943.[21] Murray was practicing a strategy that would be implemented nationally seventeen years later. In her autobiography, she consistently expresses gratification at seeing such effective action, recognizing that her effort and that of her friends was the right action at the wrong time.[22] As a law student, it was Murray who presented a strategy to overturn *Plessy v. Ferguson*, a strategy roundly mocked by her (entirely male) colleagues. Twenty years later, one of her professors used her paper to frame the argument before the Supreme Court that ended Jim Crow. Her generation provided tools and practices to an arsenal of creative public protest and insightful analysis that a subsequent generation, led by a charismatic young Black man, was able to then utilize: the right action at the right time.

If I have learned anything by being the priest of a historically Black parish, it is this: social change, *political* change, is an essential aspect of living the gospel in the world. This is a hard pill to swallow for white Christians. In my Episcopalian circles, *The Black Church* on PBS was heavily viewed, and for many their takeaway was the centrality of music for Black Christians.[23] Rarely mentioned was that the music often served the purpose of motivating, supporting, and advancing organized action for intentional political change. Vincent Lloyd argues that Black theology and Black practice in the United States is not only about the critique of ideologies, but social movement organizing. The Black Church has never had the luxury of not being "political" because our political system condemns them from the moment of their birth. Not being "political" is the luxury of the privileged, those who are able to flourish because the current status quo was actually created to ensure their success at the expense of the "other." Through the intellectual and organizing work of Frederick Douglass, Anna Julia Cooper, W. E. B. DuBois, and Martin Luther King Jr., Lloyd illustrates the two-way relationship between ideology critique and movement organizing. Ideology critique is often perceived as only an intellectual discipline with movement organizing is its practical application. Yet the act of applying critical ideologies through organizing also unearths, names, and challenges the ideologies, or "natural laws" currently functioning to keep Black, brown (and female) bodies in their "place."[24] As a Catholic ethicist concerned with the "right realization of universal moral ends in public life," Jaycox argues that social anger requires the civic virtues of "restorative justice, conflictual solidarity, and prophetic prudence."[25] Restorative justice engages the hard work of repair, and conflictual solidarity highlights the liberative need to seek the justice articulated and required *by the oppressed*. Strategy is not exercised only by those who seek justice, however. Over fifty years of strategic, politically savvy organizing allowed the election of an openly sexist and racist president who would appoint a Supreme Court that would overturn court precedent regarding the rights of women to make reproductive choices. Solidarity requires that the privileged accompany, listen to, and follow the lead of the oppressed, and it is clear that the denial of abortion rights is far more detrimental to women of color than white women. Without accompaniment that listens and follows the voices of the most vulnerable, Jaycox argues that the anger of the privileged "will degenerate into frustration, resentment, helplessness, and paternalism, and any institutional reforms it motivates are very likely to maintain the status quo rather than change it."[26]

For many white U.S. citizens, outrage may not be an intentional way to avoid engaging in social action. It may be that exact sense of frustration and helplessness that arises when one has not actually engaged in the struggle for social change. André Henry, a student of social movements, interviewed Onnesha Roychoudhuri, who reminds us that effective social change does not require a majority, it requires only a small percentage of the population.[27] We do not need to convince everyone, we do not need everyone on our side. We only need *enough*. Accompanying and listening to those who have been struggling for social change provides both the comfort of company, the reality that we are enough, and that effective and strategic change takes a long time.

The day the Supreme Court overturned *Roe v. Wade*, my social media feed erupted in outrage. I escaped to a small cafe to (re)write this essay. I found myself sitting next to a table of three queer women. They joked with the waiter who gave them a choice of sides.

"Thanks for respecting our dignity," they quip. I laugh out loud, and comment about how low our bar for dignity has just become. They wryly laugh and go back to their conversation.

"Things are better," they say, "even if they aren't great." They cite one bit of changed history after another: Blacks aren't enslaved, women can vote, many have healthcare. Not perfect, but better.

"We see that the arc of justice is long." I love that even a mangled version of this quote, that "the moral arc of the universe is long, but it bends toward justice" is part of coffee table conversations.

The butch dyke agrees.

The Black woman agrees.

The J. Jill model agrees.

They start strategizing:

"You know, reservations are sovereign, right? So what if they provide family planning services?"

"Well, they are sovereign as long as they are recognized by the federal government."

"So, we need to get them recognized."

Given the subsequent Supreme Court decision that clearly undercuts the sovereignty of tribal land, this may not be a viable strategy. But strategy for the long haul is what we need: strategic, creative, and thoughtful plans engage in restorative justice through conflictual solidarity.

The reality is, my parish is small, aged, and struggling. I can't preach outrage about what is happening because my people experience the outrage in their bones more completely than I ever will. I can't preach as if they don't know the history, because they lived and live the history of racism every day. I would just be telling them what they already know: that emancipation is incomplete. Declared by Abraham Lincoln on September 22, 1862, effective January 1, 1863, but not announced in the (then) geographically isolated Texas until June 19, 1865, the emancipation celebrated on Juneteenth continues to elude us in a land where the law is used to justify terrorizing brown and Black bodies.

But these people, my people, they press me to ask the next set of questions, the set of questions white folks don't want to ask because the answers might demand of us things we are not willing to sacrifice: What does responsibility in the face of racist relationships actually look like? What must be repaired? And who must do the repairing?

NOTES

1. This essay is a revised and expanded version of my post "Outrage: To Whom Are We Responsible?," *WIT: Women in Theology*, June 19, 2018, https://womenintheology.org/2018/06/19/outrage-to-whom-are-we-responsible/.

2. Kelly Brown Douglas, *Stand Your Ground: Black Bodies and the Justice of God* (Maryknoll, NY: Orbis Books, 2015), 68ff.

3. More accurately, my friend shared with me the phrase of his friend, a "genuine diesel dyke who has been doing community activism for decades."

4. Michael P. Jaycox, "The Civic Virtues of Social Anger: A Critically Reconstructed Normative Ethic for Public Life," *Journal of the Society of Christian Ethics* 36, no. 1 (2016): 125.

5. See Nussbaum's work and responses from Christian ethicists. In particular, see Diana Fritz Cates, "Conceiving Emotions: Martha Nussbaum's Upheavals of Thought," *Journal of Religious Ethics* 31, no. 2 (2003): 325–41; Diana Fritz Cates, "You Deserve to Suffer for What You Did," *Journal of Religious Ethics* 46, no. 4 (2018): 771–82; Timothy P. (Timothy Patrick) Jackson, "Not Far From the Kingdom: Martha Nussbaum on Anger and Forgiveness," *Journal of Religious Ethics* 46, no. 4 (2018): 749–70; Martha Craven Nussbaum, *Upheavals of Thought: The Intelligence of Emotions* (Cambridge: Cambridge University Press, 2001); Martha Craven Nussbaum, *Anger and Forgiveness: Resentment, Generosity, Justice* (Oxford: Oxford University Press, 2016).

6. Michael P. Jaycox, "Nussbaum, Anger, and Racial Justice: On the Epistemological and Eschatological Limitations of White Liberalism," *Political Theology* 21, no. 5 (2020): 415–33. Here, Jaycox is significantly influenced by Charles W. Mills's incisive work.

7. See David Bradshaw, "Why We Need Nature," *Public Orthodoxy*, September 10, 2019, https://publicorthodoxy.org/2019/09/10/why-we-need-nature/; and my response, "Fat Pills and Sexbots: A Serious Orthodox Engagement with Sexual Diversity," *WIT: Women in Theology*, September 16, 2019, https://womenintheology.org/2019/09/16/fat-pills-and-sexbots-a-serious-orthodox-engagement-with-sexual-diversity/.

8. Rebecca Traister, "Fury Is a Political Weapon. And Women Need to Wield It," *New York Times*, September 29, 2018, https://

www.nytimes.com/2018/09/29/opinion/sunday/fury-is-a-political-weapon-and-women-need-to-wield-it.html.

9. Traister, "Fury Is a Political Weapon."
10. Jaycox, "Civic Virtues of Social Anger," 124.
11. Jaycox, "Civic Virtues of Social Anger," 129.
12. Jaycox, "Civic Virtues of Social Anger," 130.
13. Traister elucidates the many ways in which women's anger has been utilized for social change in her book *Good and Mad: The Revolutionary Power of Women's Anger* (New York: Simon & Schuster, 2019).
14. Katie Grimes. "Trauma at the Border: Is the Bond between Criminalized Parent and Child Sacred as Well?," *WIT: Women in Theology*, June 18, 2018, https://womenintheology.org/2018/06/18/trauma-at-the-border-is-the-bond-between-criminalized-parent-and-child-sacred-as-well/.
15. Tisha M. Rajendra, *Migrants and Citizens: Justice and Responsibility in the Ethics of Immigration* (Grand Rapids, MI: Eerdmans, 2017).
16. María Teresa Dávila, "Discussing Racial Justice in Light of 2016: Black Lives Matter, a Trump Presidency, and the Continued Struggle for Justice," *Journal of Religious Ethics* 45, no. 4 (2017): 761–92.
17. Dávila, "Discussing Racial Justice in Light of 2016," 785.
18. Jennifer Harvey, *Dear White Christians* (Grand Rapids, MI: Eerdmans, 2020).
19. Amaryah Shaye Jones-Armstrong, personal correspondence, August 30, 2017.
20. The incident of near-rape was discovered in an essay written by Ms. Parks, found in her effects after her death, and can be seen at the Library of Congress online exhibit, "Rosa Parks: In Her Own Words." ("Childhood Encounter," Rosa Parks: In Her Own Words, Library of Congress, https://www.loc.gov/exhibitions/rosa-parks-in-her-own-words/about-this-exhibition/early-life-and-activism/childhood-encounter/). It is mentioned by Traister in her book, and covered by Marylou Tousignant, "For Rosa Parks, Standing Up to Injustice Started When She Was a Kid," *Washington Post*, February 3, 2020, https://www.washingtonpost.com/lifestyle/kidspost/for-rosa-parks-standing-up-to-injustice-started-when-she-was-a-kid/2020/02/03/8caaa6f2-387e-11ea-bb7b-265f4554af6d_story.html.

21. "Pauli Murray Organizes Howard Student Sit-Ins," SNCC Digital Gateway, accessed June 30, 2022, https://snccdigital.org/events/pauli-murray-organizes-howard-student-sit-ins/.

22. Pauli Murray, *Song in a Weary Throat: Memoir of an American Pilgrimage* (New York: Harper & Row, 1987).

23. See *The Black Church*, PBS, https://www.pbs.org/show/black-church/.

24. Vincent W. Lloyd, *Black Natural Law* (New York: Oxford University Press, 2016).

25. Jaycox, "Civic Virtues of Social Anger," 131.

26. Jaycox, "Civic Virtues of Social Anger," 136.

27. "Becoming the Majority We Already Are with Onnesha Roychoudhuri," *Hope and Hard Pills*, https://pca.st/z7vf3hca. See Onnesha Roychoudhuri, *The Marginalized Majority: Claiming Our Power in a Post-truth America* (Brooklyn: Melville House, 2018).

8

UNHOLY TRINITY

Incel Ideology, Complementarian Theology, and Toxic Masculinity

Alexandria Barbera and Allison Murray

Introduction

As Canadians, we both paid very close attention to the coverage of the Toronto Van Attack, a horrific act of misogynistic terror that took place in April 2018. Ten people were killed and another sixteen injured by a twenty-five-year-old man who chose to drive a rented cargo van down a kilometer of sidewalk on a thoroughfare in the north end of the city, targeting pedestrians as he went. In June of 2022, the perpetrator was found guilty of twenty-six charges related to the attack and was sentenced to life in prison with no possibility for parole for at least twenty-five years. Before committing his crime, he posted a message on his Facebook page indicating his actions were driven by misogyny, making links between his violent rampage and those committed by other so-called incels. Some accounts suggested he targeted women specifically as he set about his killing spree (though Toronto police downplayed this possibility). As media reports about men's rights activists and incels made their rounds, this terrifying act brought viewpoints bred in some of the Internet's darkest corners into the public eye. As we each took in the reporting on these movements, we saw many assumptions that were strikingly similar to what we had found in our separate research on complementarian theology within contemporary evangelicalism.[1] Over the course of this chapter, we will compare the assumptions and rhetoric of incels and complementarians, highlighting areas of overlap and agreement.[2] Our core argument is this: The existence of ideological parallels between these two seemingly unrelated movements shows their common underlying foundation of toxic notions about masculinity. Toxic masculinity has various manifestations that undermine the flourishing and safety of people of all genders and its presence in Christian spaces needs to be addressed.

It is important to clarify some of the key terms in this essay before we launch our analysis. First: *toxic masculinity*. This term developed in the social sciences in the 1980s and has undergone some renovation since. Toxic masculinity can be understood as a "constellation of socially regressive male traits that serve to foster domination, the devaluation of women, homophobia, and wanton violence."[3] Toxic masculinity surfaces as a defense of (some) male individuals and hegemonic masculinity when an individual or group understands their identity or societal position to be under threat. Perceived threats can include the existence of gay people, the absence of sexual activity, independent women, social isolation, the legal system, and more. Within this constellation of toxic masculinity, the assumed boundaries of masculinity are aggressively policed, and a rigid binary of male and female is posited.

Our second term of note is *incel*, a portmanteau of "involuntary celibacy." The label first surfaced among a group of "late bloomers" who longed for romantic connections and healthy sex lives but found themselves unlucky in the dating world. The first online message board for involuntary celibates was started by a queer woman in the 1990s. This early online community attracted people of all genders, sexual orientations, and levels of social aptitude, and offered encouragement, dating advice, sexual education, and other forms of mutual support. In more recent years, however, the demographics and tone of incel message boards has shifted dramatically (much to the chagrin of the first message board's founder[4]). While the early community was marked by diversity, in the last decade incel message boards have been dominated by young, lonely, straight men fixated on social hierarchies. Meeting together in online message boards to share their sexual woes, incels have spun narratives that cast themselves as victims. They see sexual relationships with women as something to which they are entitled and of which they are unjustly being deprived. Reporters and scholars who write about incel culture have demonstrated that incel discourse is rife with misogyny, antifeminism, white supremacy, and violent levels of male entitlement.[5]

And finally, *complementarianism*. This term refers to a highly gendered theological anthropology that emerged within white American evangelicalism in the 1970s as a rejoinder to Second Wave feminism and its insistence that gender roles are the product of socialization and therefore open to revision. Complementarianism purports that men and women innately possess opposing-yet-complementary characteristics, drives, temperaments, and desires. The divinely ordained differences complementarian writers believe exist between men and women mean that each should fulfill separate, complementary roles in the home, in the church, and in society. For example, men should lead, and women should submit; men should provide for their families economically, while women should eschew paid labor and devote their time to caring for the home and children; men will be logical, women will be emotional; and so on. Supporting its views with a narrow biblical hermeneutic, the highly prescriptive complementarian system envisions everyone to be straight and cisgender. Proponents present its teachings as a framework that will insulate faithful families from relational strife, divorce, ending up with queer children, and a myriad of other dissatisfactions they assume come from straying from God's design for human beings.

Christians who hold complementarian beliefs would certainly denounce the violent behavior of the Toronto attacker and likely reject any comparisons between his gruesome act and their own (sexist) theology. But regardless of complementarianism's ostensible rejection of violence against women and extremist behavior, it shares some of the key features of toxic masculinity that are identifiable within incel discourse. Common threads woven in the two discourses include a disparaging of feminism; understanding themselves as a persecuted minority; fixation on hierarchies and boundary policing; appeals to natural law; and presenting women's bodies as pacifiers of unethical or violent male behavior. The intricate webs of evangelical sexism and incel ideology are spun of many common threads.

Practicing Theology

Feminism: A Common Enemy

In studying complementarian teachings and reading incel materials one quickly notices that members of these two groups share a common enemy: feminism, or more rightly, something they call feminism that evidences a misunderstanding and misrepresentation of feminist goals, values and social influence. According to both complementarians and members of these misogynist online communities, feminists are responsible for the downward turn of society as its ideology offers a "one-way ticket to social anarchy,"[6] and disrupts "natural" hierarchies between men and women. Both groups imagine a prefeminist past as a golden age to which we should return. Beyond its "Bible-centered" rationale, complementarianism regularly foments an antifeminist ethos to sustain itself. Feminism is demonized for all sorts of social evils that are harmful to God's supposed plan for men and women. Feminism is portrayed as an outside secular force that corrupts God's created order and threatens to disrupt the continuity of tradition, biblical teaching, and faithful Christian witness. Feminism, then, is an offense to that which is natural, biblical, and divinely revealed. When it is not viewed with menace and suspicion, its hermeneutics are portrayed as methodologically inferior.

The confidence with which complementarians proclaim feminism's foreign (and therefore heretical) status to Christianity is both ill-informed and highly unimaginative. Refusal to maximize the interpretive potential of standout women of the Bible or blocking any feminist attempts to wrestle with Paul's contradictory statements regarding women (cf. Gal 3:28 and 1 Cor 14:35) signals fidelity not to Scripture but to a narrow and oppressive hermeneutic. Engaging with history, too, troubles the feminism-is-sinful/patriarchy-is-biblical dichotomy when we remember that many early women's rights activists were also professing, committed Christians. Even more to the point, complementarian antifeminism can only exist by suppressing or discrediting the work of women writers, scholars, and activists working *today* who claim both Christian and feminist commitments. Instead of seeing their feminism as a capitulation to secularism, postmodernism, or any other form of blasphemy, we should take seriously these women's assertions that faith and feminism are compatible (or, more radically, that the latter is actually strengthened by the former). Ironically, complementarians' rejection and mischaracterization of feminism are identical to that of incels, men's rights activists, and other groups that denounce feminism. It seems then that antifeminism is not a uniquely Christian position after all.

Embattled Men

Both groups create a narrative that suggests that the mainstream way of seeing things is wrong and that a better way is possible when one views the world through the lenses they provide. These groups cast men and manhood as embattled and provide "red pill" solutions to their perceived problems. In incel discourse men are victims of a society that diminishes their power and disincentivizes women from engaging with them. Incels believe themselves, and all men, to be oppressed by the feminist mainstream. Although not surprising, incel communities never seem willing to confront the ways in which their thinking victimizes *themselves*, placing them at the mercy of women's willingness to provide them with sexual opportunities.

Both incel messaging and complementarian teachings tend to frame their adherents as a minority group with all the right answers in a world that has got it wrong. From the complementarian perspective, the world at large—seduced by feminism—has forgotten the separate and distinct roles divinely assigned to men and women. The system portrays male headship as both positive and necessary, prefers that mothers rear their children full-time and remain out of the paid workforce, and enjoys boundary policing between the genders.

Male complementarian authors routinely point to the denigration of masculinity in recent decades, arguing that "under the assault of modern culture and feminist ideology, bold images of manhood... have been silenced."[7] As a result, boys are punished for manliness and "young men are taught to apologize for their masculinity."[8] In both gendered discourses, men are victims who are disenfranchised by our society's recent "unnatural," shift in gender roles and expectations.

Practicing Theology

Hierarchies and Boundaries

Both of these variants of toxic masculinity present masculinity as fragile. In each worldview men need women to act in specific ways for men to feel secure in their maleness. Men also need other men to act in specific ways to maintain the "purity" and "integrity" of masculinity. Filtered through these lenses, a man gets the idea that—in order to be confident in his maleness—he must avoid transgressive behaviors like wearing pink or reading books authored by women. These individual choices threaten to break down the imagined "sacred" or "natural" barriers between masculinity and femininity. Furthermore, men are also expected to ridicule these behaviors in others to ensure other men are not threatening that boundary. Major transgressions, like being a stay-at-home father or loving other men, are to be critiqued, punished, and discouraged.

The main rhetorical strategy of this brand of evangelical sexism is undoubtedly a hyperreliance on the biblical text to answer any and every question pertaining to even the most minute, innocuous aspects of our gendered lives: Is it biblical for men to enjoy singing hymns that focus too much on love? What damage is done to a woman's feminine beauty if *she* pursues a man romantically? These are minor examples of the larger evangelical tendency to emphasize the "Bible-centered" nature of the complementarian worldview as a whole. Their arguments have been most effective in more general "family values" discussions, since it is hard to conceal how trivial it is to claim there is a biblically sanctioned worship style that godly men prefer singing. But as Dave Murrow laments in *Why Men Hate Going to Church*, the old style of masculine worship was "formal, corporate, and emotionless" and, even more crucially, served a *purpose* to "extol God" rather than cultivate intimacy. This exemplifies a purposeless agenda he associates with the static nature of femininity and the "touchy-feely" character of contemporary worship.[9] This is an evangelical example of that transgressive behavior crucial to the logic of toxic masculinity more broadly, where men's personal choices are scrutinized for their (in)ability to uphold the gendered prescriptions needed to be seen as an ideal man.

These instances verify an ideological commitment to the core assumptions of toxic masculinity, which itself depends on an overarching binary logic governing male and female identity in complementarian circles. It is a style of thinking that is a mainstay of every community that espouses some version of cultural sexism (incels included). The pettiness of dividing music and dating preferences into male/female compartments is likely not lost on the more prominent leaders of the complementarian movement. This inevitably compels them to focus most of their exegetical efforts on marriage and sexuality, and indeed these weightier topics are where conservative-leaning Christians are most eager to entertain sexist theology. Their ideas are given divine authority mainly through policing biblical interpretation, especially in their appeals to "perspicuity" or the plain meaning of a passage. This allows them to argue for the alleged autonomy of complementarian "truths" that, although conforming to historic Christian teaching, transcend church tradition in their view. Of course, this is disingenuous—just as it is disingenuous for these neo-patriarchalists to claim that they derive support for their ideas solely from the Bible and not from naturalistic fallacies. The key is to ground their belief system in some original order of nature that is, crucially, distinctly *theological* in character.

The Nature of Things

In complementarian teaching there is a good amount of flirtation with natural theology, even though those two words rarely (if ever) appear in the discourse of prominent conservative evangelical publications. For example, we can see how this appeal to the "naturalness" of binary gender roles appears in the writing of John Piper, one of complementarianism's longest-standing and highest-profile proponents. "Manhood and womanhood are the beautiful handiwork of a good and loving God," proclaims Piper. "He designed our differences."[10] The entire premise of the "biblical manhood and womanhood" project is reclaiming a gendered relationship between men and women that is coherent with God's "handiwork," that is, the natural, created order. This natural and absolute binary of manhood and womanhood is, functionally, a reassertion of nineteenth-century gender essentialism where men and women are thought to embody opposite (and noninterchangeable) characteristics, temperaments, and proclivities. Here is a further example of this dynamic from author Stu Weber:

> Among the ancient Hebrew words for man is one meaning "piercer."...While the anatomical or sexual elements are clear, the force of the words is much larger in scope....The visible is a metaphor for the invisible. The tangible speaks for the intangible. At his core a man is an initiator—a piercer, one who penetrates, moves forward, advances toward the horizon, leads.[11]

The natural order, for Weber and other complementarians, permeates every element of our essence. As for Piper, male/female differences "are not mere physiological prerequisites for sexual union" but "they are profound" and "go to the root of our personhood," influencing our personalities, skills, and roles.[12]

Similarly, incel ideology also makes its own (twisted and uninformed) appeals to nature. As noted by social science researcher Angus Lindsay, within incel communities "biological deterministic arguments and language" appear in assertions of "natural differences and propensities between men and women." These differences are tied to a gendered (and often racialized) hierarchy.[13] Journalist Amelia Tait observed a similar pattern in her own interviews with ex-incels. By drawing on a combination of biological determinism and distortions of evolutionary psychology, Tait noted members of online incel groups tend to express a misogyny "justified by one of their favorite acronyms, AWALT: 'all women are like that.'"[14] Assuming there is a particular, immutable, and essentialist "nature" shared by all women is directly tied to the dehumanization of women in the incel framework.

Within these both groups, a misunderstanding of human social evolution perpetuates the idea that society has undermined the "natural" way of things. Their rigid understandings of what women are "for" based on what is "natural" are used to justify misogynist views, sexist church governance policies, chauvinistic home arrangements, and legions of other prescriptions and proscriptions on women's (and men's) behavior. In inceldom and complementarianism we find the same entitlement to a vast spectrum of women's labour—emotional, sexual, and procreative labour in particular. To members of these groups the assumed perspicuity of God's or nature's design makes the rightness of their perspective obvious to any observant, rational creature. A social order that undermines this essentialist model (such as one promoted by many liberal feminists) is pronounced illogical and harmful because it goes against the natural, God-ordained order of things. Aligning one's theology or ideology with nature, especially if words like *creation* and *original design* are used, is an effective way to imbue it with authority.

The Salve of Sex

One of the most troubling commonalities shared by complementarians and incels is the notion that sexual access to women's bodies will "cure" men's psychosocial ailments. Both groups believe that regular partnered sexual activity will prevent men from behaving badly. In various letters, manifestos, rants, and screeds shared by incels who have gone on to commit large-scale acts of violence, readers will note a recurring theme: lack of female sexual partners has left perpetrators feeling worthless, rejected, and enraged. These men express a sense that they are entitled to female sexual partners and blame women for withholding the sense of validation and soothed egos they believe would stem from an active sex life. An incel who went on a rampage at University of California, Santa Barbara, in 2014 described himself as someone "forced to endure an existence of loneliness, rejection, and unfulfilled desires."[15] Calling his ongoing virginal status "an injustice, a crime," he set out to "punish" female students at his university campus. This twenty-two-year-old man went on to kill six people, injure fourteen others, and end his own life. In so doing he also became a hero and an inspiration to other incels, including the 2018 Toronto perpetrator. The incel argument goes that if women had opened their bodies to these men, these men would not be committing atrocious acts of violence.

The same patriarchal assumptions in incel communities that excuse violence as a by-product of stalled sexual expression are fully operational in complementarian discourse. In much writing produced by complementarian authors, access to women's bodies—specifically, a husband's access to his wife's body—plays a similar role. Wives "providing" their husbands with sex are safeguarding their husbands from temptation and poor choices.

In complementarian literature, men are presented as inherently sexual creatures who will, by default, trespass social and sexual boundaries if their sexual needs go unfulfilled. Emerson Eggerichs, in his 2009 best-selling complementarian marriage manual *Love and Respect*, tells his readers that "men are often lured into affairs because they are sexually deprived at home."[16] Eggerichs is voicing a consensus opinion in this statement. Across hundreds of complementarian books, regular access to sex is said to prevent adultery, emotional affairs, pornography use, child molestation, masturbation, same-sex attraction, and a whole host of other undesirable behaviors. Just as incels declare their violence would not be happening had they not been rejected sexually, the complementarian marital sexual economy links antisocial or ethically dubious sexual behavior to men's sexual deprivation.

One difference between these two discourses: with respect to incels, most of the women involved are simply going about their daily lives, unaware of the anger they are "causing" by their "neglect." In the complementarian framework women are made very aware of their role in the story and are actively told to cultivate a care and concern for their husbands' sexual needs. A respondent to a survey conducted by the authors of one such book, *Every Man's Battle: Winning the War on Sexual Temptation One Battle at a Time*, described her sex life as follows:

> [My husband's] purity is extremely important to me, so I try to meet his needs so that he goes out each day with his cup full. During the earlier years, with much energy going into childcare and with my monthly cycle, it was a lot more difficult for me to do that. There weren't too many "ideal times" when everything was just right. But that's life, and I did it anyway.[17]

Ensconced in "purity" language, complementarian advice books, like *Every Man's Battle*, repeatedly present a wife's participation in sexual relations as an activity that keeps her husband on the straight and narrow path of fidelity, rather than as something she might enjoy for her own sake.

Both incel and complementarian discourses paint the unsexed man as a victim, one who can point to others in blame for his violent or antisocial behaviors. In one of the more egregious patterns of what philosopher Kate Manne has dubbed "himpathy"—that is, "the disproportionate or inappropriate sympathy extended to a male perpetrator over his similarly or less privileged female targets or victims,"[18]—complementarian books frequently employ rhetoric that transfers culpability from the male sexual transgressor to his wife. While incels express a general (unfounded) entitlement to sex, complementarian authors will make appeals to spiritual and theological justification husbands' entitlement to sexual intercourse with their wives. The complementarian system portrays sex, on a spiritual level, as an activity that enables the ongoing sanctification of the male soul; it fuels him toward perfection.[19] Here is one example from complementarian author Elyse Fitzpatrick:

> Although most women recognize that they probably don't have sex as much as they should, we rarely think about this abstinence as sin. When we refuse our husband's attentions, we're actually robbing him...of what we owe him. In addition to stealing from him what's rightfully his, we're also exposing him and ourselves to unnecessary temptation. As a wife who's been called to help her husband, this is one of the major ways I can fulfill that calling. If I ignore Phil's needs, then I'm answerable for the storm of temptation with which he has to struggle.[20]

The parallels to incel discourse are easily apparent here. As the attacker in Isla Vista called the absence of sex in his life "an injustice, a crime," here we see Fitzpatrick refer to wifely abstinence as "robbing" and "stealing." Men/husbands are owed sex. Women/wives bear the blame for whatever consequences might arise "because" of an unfulfilled male libido. Should their husbands commit an act of violence or allow his sexuality to find expression outside of their marriage, female readers of complementarian books are proactively primed to see themselves as the "real" perpetrators and their husbands the victims of their frigidity.

When too much is expected of sex (when it is needed to "save"), too much is expected of women's bodies. The blatant violence of the incel movement is easy to see, but it is important to recognize the more subtle, quotidian violence embedded within the complementarian sexual paradigm. By centering male sexual fulfillment women's desires are completely erased. This framework erodes bodily integrity and any emphasis on consent because it places blame and derision on wives who "deny" their husbands. When a woman is told denying her husband sex will make her responsible for any sins he commits as a "result" of sexual dissatisfaction it creates a strong-arm environment, undermining the freedom needed for enthusiastic consent. It also transfers blame from the sinner to his spouse, as though somehow men are less theologically culpable for their transgressions. What is veiled as affirming the good of married sex is at its heart sexual coercion with a theological gloss.

Conclusion

Entrenchment within either of these ideologies diminishes both women and men's flourishing—whether the result is an event worthy of the evening news, a man feeling like violence is the only response to feelings of insecurity, or a woman quietly weeping at home as she interprets her husband's sins as the result of her own failings.

It is hard to deny that, overall, complementarianism is a less serious, more genteel version of incel thinking. But genteel toxicity is still toxic. It is perhaps even more insidious because its mask of respectability hides its discursive damage. Like the white moderate bemoaned by the Reverend Doctor Martin Luther King Jr.,[21] the gentle toxicity of the complementarian worldview might pose as significant a hurdle to the well-being of our society as its more aggressive secular counterparts (such as the incel movement). In some cases, these groups speak in one voice; in others, the complementarian expression of toxic masculinity is the incel movement's gentler, less crude echo. This raises several important questions not only about the connection between complementarianism and toxic masculinity, but also about the influence of the (supposedly) secular culture on faith communities, who largely deny this influence and indeed work tirelessly to carve out a political identity in opposition to that culture. Arguably, it is this culture versus Christian mentality that leads many of evangelicalism's prominent leaders to justify their misogynistic theology in the name of protecting this "pure" Christian worldview and identity, and especially to restrict as much as possible the influence of feminism, which they associate with godlessness and secularity.

There is a compelling argument that toxic notions about masculinity are at play in acts of violence (such as the Toronto Van Attack), when women are killed by their male partners, or in horrific mass shootings. These incidents spark a near-liturgical response in North American culture, as various officials and pundits often denounce such tragedy or terrorism but fail to address the root causes of widespread societal lament. "When people jump to blame mental illness instead of misogyny for this demonstrable pattern [of men committing acts of mass violence]," writes journalist Aditi Natasha Kini, "they underestimate/undercut the violence of misogyny and undermine the safety of women. There is no diagnosis that all mass shooters share. Sexual entitlement is not in the DSM—but it's chock full in unchecked online communities [where incels gather and share]."[22] Naming toxic masculinity and the negative behaviors it engenders is something both the church and the world need to get better at.

Other blog posts on *WIT* have unpacked how theological principles give us "tool kits" to understand the world around us.[23] There are plenty of examples of theological tool kits acting as barriers to seeing ourselves and our world clearly. Theology and church cultures that undergird toxic masculinity serve as another prime example of faulty tool kits. We need to call out the tools. We all do—but especially men. Men need to learn to recognize the toxic notions of masculinity they have internalized themselves and call out manifestations of toxic masculinity when they see them. We need men to invest and risk their social capital for this. Harness that gender-policing bent you might have had socialized into you and start to turn it in on itself. Stop equating manhood with anything that hints at toxic masculinity and correct your fellow men when you see them doing it. It is not always as obvious as some of the usual suspects often make it. Sometimes it is a subtle joke in a sermon, a twisted parallel in the introduction to a Bible study, an allusion in a wedding ceremony, or passing comments in coffee hour chatter. Just as these ideas spread in online communities that normalize belief, these ideas are perpetuated in our theological and religious cultures. Pushing back against that is where we can start to make changes. It will not be easy but could very well save lives.

NOTES

1. This chapter is a synthesis and expansion of two posts we coauthored for *Women in Theology* in 2018. See Alexandria Barbera and Allison Murray, "Unholy Trinity: Incel Ideology, Complementarian Theology, and Toxic Masculinity: Part I," *WIT: Women in Theology*, October 23, 2018, https://womenintheology.org/2018/10/23/unholy-trinity-incel-ideology-complementarian-theology-and-toxic-masculinity-part-i/; and Alexandria Barbera and Allison Murray, "Unholy Trinity: Incel Ideology, Complementarian Theology, and Toxic Masculinity: Part II," *WIT: Women in Theology*, October 26, 2018, https://womenintheology.org/2018/10/26/unholy-trinity-incel-ideology-complementarian-theology-and-toxic-masculinity-part-ii/.

2. For more on complementarian theology, see Allison Murray's chapter, "Unpacking 'Biblical Womanhood': Theological Nostalgia, Gender, and History."

3. Terry A. Kupers, "Toxic Masculinity as a Barrier to Mental Health Treatment in Prison," *Journal of Clinical Psychology* 61, no. 6 (June 2005): 714.

4. Ashifa Kassam, "Woman behind 'Incel' Says Angry Men Hijacked Her Word 'as a Weapon of War,'" *The Guardian*, April 26, 2018, https://www.theguardian.com/world/2018/apr/25/woman-who-invented-incel-movement-interview-toronto-attack.

5. Kate Manne, "Involuntary: On the Entitlement to Admiration," in *Entitled: How Male Privilege Hurts Women* (New York: Crown, 2020), 14–32; Aditi Natasha Kini, "How Reddit Is Used to Indoctrinate Young Men into Becoming Misogynists," *Vice*, November 15, 2017, https://www.vice.com/en_ca/article/gyj3yw/how-reddit-is-used-to-indoctrinate-young-men-into-becoming-misogynists.

6. Mary Pride, *The Way Home: Beyond Feminism and Back to Reality* (Wheaton, IL: Crossway Books, 1985), xi–xii.

7. Robert Lewis, *Raising a Modern-Day Knight: A Father's Role in Guiding His Son to Authentic Manhood*, Kindle edition (Carol Stream, IL: Tyndale House, 2007), 682/2506.

8. Voddie Baucham, *What He Must Be...If He Wants to Marry My Daughter* (Wheaton, IL: Crossway Books, 2009), 202–3.

9. Dave Murrow, *Why Men Hate Going to Church* (Nashville: Thomas Nelson, 2011), 15–18; 70–76.

10. John Piper, "Created Male and Female by a Loving God," *Desiring God*, https://www.desiringgod.org/topics/manhood-womanhood.

11. Stu Weber, *Tender Warrior: God's Intention for a Man* (Sisters, OR: Multnomah Books, 1993), 44.

12. Piper, "Created Male and Female by a Loving God."

13. Angus Lindsay, "Swallowing the Black Pill: Involuntary Celibates' (Incels) Anti Feminism within Digital Society," *International Journal for Crime, Justice and Social Democracy* 11, no. 1 (March 1, 2022): 219, https://doi.org/10.5204/ijcjsd.2138.

14. Amelia Tait, "Spitting Out the Red Pill: Former Misogynists Reveal How They Were Radicalised Online," *New Statesman*, February 28, 2017, https://www.newstatesman.com/science-tech/2017/02/reddit-the-red-pill-interview-how-misogyny-spreads-online.

15. As quoted in Manne, *Entitled*, 15.

16. Emerson Eggerichs, *Love and Respect: The Love She Most Desires, the Respect He Desperately Needs* (Nashville: Thomas Nelson Publishers, 2004), 253.

17. Stephen Arterburn, Fred Stoeker, and Mike Yorkey, *Every Man's Battle: Winning the War on Sexual Temptation One Victory at a Time* (Colorado Springs, CO: WaterBrook Press, 2000), 79.

18. Manne, *Entitled*, 36.

19. For more on this line of argument we would refer readers to this excellent work: Amy DeRogatis, *Saving Sex: Sexuality and Salvation in American Evangelicalism* (New York: Oxford University Press, 2014). For an example of evangelical authors trying to combat the dominant complementarian portrayal of sexual intimacy, see Sheila Wray Gregoire, *The Great Sex Rescue: The Lies You've Been Taught and How to Recover What God Intended* (Grand Rapids, MI: Baker Books, 2021).

20. Elyse Fitzpatrick, *Helper by Design: God's Perfect Plan for Women in Marriage* (Chicago: Moody Publishers, 2003), 105.

21. Martin Luther King Jr., "Letter from a Birmingham Jail," April 16, 1963, accessed at *African Studies Center—University of*

Pennsylvania, https://www.africa.upenn.edu/Articles_Gen/Letter_Birmingham.html.

22. Kini, "How Reddit Is Used to Indoctrinate."

23. Allison Murray, "How Our Theology Keeps Us Racist," *WIT: Women in Theology*, July 15, 2017, https://womenintheology.org/2017/07/15/how-our-theology-keeps-us-racist/.

9

DISCERNING THE "SIGNS OF THE TIMES" AND DOING PUBLIC THEOLOGY IN AN EVANGELICAL CONTEXT

Mandy Rodgers-Gates

> The Church has always had the duty of scrutinizing the signs of the times and of interpreting them in the light of the Gospel.
>
> *Gaudium et Spes* 4[1]

A week after the events of January 6, 2021, Al Mohler—president of a prominent Southern Baptist seminary and an important leader in the Southern Baptist community—responded to the Christian symbolism used in the attack on the Capitol by seeking to articulate the dangers of nationalism and to make distinctions between it and an appropriate kind of patriotism. He went so far as to identify what was seen on January 6 as "Christian nationalism of an idolatrous sort," while denying that such an "idolatrous fusion" characterized "mainstream evangelical Christianity."[2] However, less than eighteen months later, Mohler, like many other Christians and prominent conservative voices, had come to embrace the Christian nationalist label: "We have the left routinely speaking of me and of others as Christian nationalists, as if we're supposed to be running from that....I'm not about to run from that."[3] How are those doing public theology with and for white evangelicals to respond to such an embrace of Christian nationalism? How ought white evangelical pastors and leaders respond?

I propose in this chapter one resource for addressing the problem of Christian nationalism among white evangelical Christians: the theological approach of interpreting the "signs of the times." I offer here a modest proposal for evangelicals to engage with the global church along these lines, in order to develop their own approach to this component of the church's life and witness, one that allows for a more self-critical engagement with social-historical events and trends. Such an engagement is needed due to evangelicals' neglect of an explicit and intentional approach to interpreting the signs of the times, one that is grounded in a christological hermeneutic of cruciformity. As a result, Christian nationalism has taken the place of a gospel-centered discernment of historical events, such that its ideological narratives and myths have become the lens through which many (though not all) white evangelicals interpret the signs of the times. In the following pages, I will first develop a few of the key insights and aids that a theological approach to the "signs of the times" offers, drawing primarily from Latin American sources post–Vatican II, then I conclude with the implications for the evangelical embrace of Christian nationalism.

As a white evangelical born and raised in the United States, a winding path led me to undertake a dissertation on Mons. Óscar Romero, archbishop of El Salvador from 1977 to 1980. Extreme inequality, political conflict, violence, and persecution against the church characterized El Salvador during Romero's tenure as archbishop. His assassination in March 1980 by those carrying out the wishes of right-wing elites coincided with the beginning of a civil war that would last more than a decade. The more I studied Romero, the more his ability to speak to the circumstances and events of his moment in the light of the Christian gospel drew me in. Romero is known for including in his sermons lengthy reflections on the events of the week. By his final months, Romero was dedicating the latter half of his messages to these events (around thirty minutes out of a one-hour sermon). Romero included these details in part because reliable sources of information were scarce at that moment in Salvadoran society. In an extreme situation of media bias—the powerful and wealthy controlled communication channels—the church was able to provide a counternarrative and deploy supporting evidence due to its ubiquitous presence in remote areas and the trust it had earned from the people.

But Romero's purpose in his commentary went beyond simply reporting facts. Romero intended to provide a unique perspective, one only the church could offer, on important happenings in the life of his country. What kinds of happenings? Romero focused particularly on instances of suffering, violence, and death. Anyone familiar with the El Salvador of the 1970s and 1980s may think this focus unremarkable. Romero's motivation for such a focus, however, was theological: a christological hermeneutic for interpreting the signs of the times. This christological hermeneutic, discussed in more detail below, entails a focus on suffering because (1) Christ reveals to us that God is present in a particular way among those who suffer and (2) suffering and death are the consequences of sin, exposed as such by sin's primary and foremost victim, the crucified Jesus.

As I studied his sermons, I found that Romero's engagement with the "signs" of his own context was bidirectional. That is, while Romero thought it his duty to shine a gospel light on current circumstances, he *also* allowed these events to shape his approach to the Scriptures for the day and whatever pastoral theme he was expounding on. The suffering of the Salvadoran people and the violence that surrounded him impacted Romero most deeply. Furthermore, this impact was not limited to his preaching. In the address he gave at the University of Louvain (Belgium) upon receipt of an honorary doctorate in February 1980, Romero articulated the bidirectional nature of the Salvadoran church's engagement with the poor—for Romero, the central sign to be interpreted in Salvadoran society—and what impact their situation of suffering had on the church's theology and ministry. This approach, he stated,

> has clearly arisen from [the archdiocese's] faith conviction. The transcendence of the gospel has guided us in our judgment and in our action. Out of our faith we have judged

> the social and political situations. But on the other hand it is also true that precisely in the process of adopting that position before the socio-political reality as it is, that same faith has been deepening, the Gospel itself has been revealing its riches.[4]

He goes on to list a few areas in which the church's faith "has been deepening": its knowledge of sin, its understanding of the incarnation, and its faith in the God of life. The bidirectional engagement Romero articulates will characterize the church's interpretation of the signs of its time when it is performing the task well: making judgments on those signs in light of the gospel, while also allowing those signs to deepen its understanding of its own belief and provide for new encounters with God.

Romero is exemplary in his embodiment of the church's task of interpreting the signs of the times, but he is not unique. He had been shaped by the Salvadoran and wider Latin American church, by the conversations and work that took place post–Vatican II. In the pages that follow, I draw from Romero and from that wider network to discuss the meaning of "the signs of the times," the purpose of interpreting them, and the criteria by which we do so. I conclude with the implications of this practice for white evangelicalism in the United States, with a particular focus on the ideology of Christian nationalism.

What Are the "Signs of the Times"?

The biblical origin of the phrase "the signs of the times" is Matthew 16:3—"You know how to interpret the appearance of the sky, but you cannot interpret the signs of the times." The church has traditionally interpreted this verse eschatologically: Jesus speaks of the second coming and is advising his listeners to pay attention to the events that foreshadow it. The phrase "the signs of the times" appeared in *Humanae Salutis*, at John XXIII's convocation of Vatican II, and then was disseminated widely via the Vatican II pastoral constitution *Gaudium et Spes*.[5] In the 1968 bishops conference at Medellín, Latin American bishops adopted the phrase, with two central addresses focused on

Discerning the "Signs of the Times"

this theme. Thus, the phrase began to take on a new life and meaning, though its use is debated and sometimes murky.

The theological basis Mons. Eduardo Pironio gives at Medellín for the task of interpreting the signs of the times is christological. He quotes *Gaudium et Spes* in its claim that Christ is the "the key, the focal point and the goal...of all human history."[6] Building on this claim, he states that it is Christ himself who "presides now over history, giving salvific content to the times that follow him."[7] Here we find two key points widely agreed upon by those who use the phrase: (1) the *christological* basis for the task of interpreting the signs of the times and (2) the idea that God is working out the salvation brought by Christ *in the midst of* human history, and not apart from it.

Given this christological basis, what counts as a sign? While the signs are often associated with major events or historical trends, Chilean theologian Jorge Costadoat insists, "These signs do not consist in cataclysms, tsunamis, droughts, and similar disasters, but rather in the response to these phenomena, via collective praxis maintained over time."[8] In this way Costadoat presses us to consider those aspects of human life and society that carry a collective moral weight, via human agency and response. If the salvation that Christ brought is being fleshed out in history by the Spirit, then we must look to human praxis for the Spirit's work. Furthermore, theologian Donal Dorr points out, "A sign is something more than an event. It is a means of communication between intelligent beings."[9] In this case, that communication is between the Spirit of God and those attending to the Spirit's voice. Dorr advocates for an understanding of the signs that "on principle" could interpret any event as such a divine communication, depending on how "in tune with the mind of Jesus" we are.[10]

I propose that we allow "the signs of the times" to include a double aspect, and this connects to my discussion of the *purpose* of interpreting the signs in the following section. This double aspect would understand that any sign—a scientific breakthrough, a mass protest movement, a particular kind of violence erupting, leadership change in a local church—any such sign can be potentially revelatory in both a positive and a negative sense. We listen for the Spirit's voice, both to see where God is already moving—where the values of the kingdom are being lived out (inside or outside the church)—and to discern where sin and evil are at work (inside or outside the church).

Practicing Theology

The importance of including both sides of interpretation leads to our next section, the purpose of interpreting these signs.

Why Interpret the Signs of the Times?

Gaudium et Spes, one of the founding documents for the concept of interpreting the signs of the times, near its beginning states this purpose:

> Thus, in language intelligible to each generation, [the church] can respond to the perennial questions which men [sic] ask about this present life and the life to come, and about the relationship of the one to the other. We must therefore recognize and understand the world in which we live, its explanations, its longings, and its often dramatic characteristics. (*GS* 4)

Here we find a focus on the church's relationship to the outside world and specifically its ability to communicate its message "in language intelligible to each generation." Such a focus could be misleading, however, if we assume that the church must make its language intelligible because of some intrinsic gap that exists between church and world, resulting from a church-world binary. One of the gifts *Gaudium et Spes* offers us is a vision of the church-world relationship that is more nuanced and complicated than the binary sometimes been promoted by Christians.

Romero understood what had changed in this relationship (or the church's understanding of it) after Vatican II, and what was at stake in such a shift:

> One of the changes of the current Church is to have broken that dichotomy, that separation between the Church and the world, because [the Church] has also understood the unity of secular history with the history of salvation. In our spirituality, in our mode of thinking as Church, there had been created [the idea] that the world was worthless, that the secular history of men was like an "in the mean-

Discerning the "Signs of the Times"

time," like a time of trial and that it was going in parallel to God's spiritual history of salvation.[11]

The history of salvation is not separable from human history. The church cannot regard the present moment nor the world as some temporary trapping of its own pilgrimage toward eternity, one easily discarded. Rather, the church knows that its own destiny is tied up with the destiny of all humanity.

Two aspects of the church's identity were critical to how Romero viewed the church's position vis-à-vis the world and therefore its task of interpreting the signs of the times: the church is both *human* and *transcendent*. To say the church is human is not merely to admit the church is prone to weakness and sin, though it certainly includes that. For Romero, to say the church is human means that all the hopes, fears, and sufferings of human society are taken up by the church as its own. When Romero was challenged as to why he performed any and every funeral, even when the background or political activity of the deceased was suspicious, he responded, "The Church has to save everything authentically human and has to accompany the pain of mothers, wives, children, and all of those that feel the human repercussions of pain, of mystery, of sin."[12] The church accompanies humanity, and that accompaniment must include humanity's experience of death. Indeed, Romero called the funerals they were celebrating in that moment—for a priest and his companions suspected of taking up arms against the government—"deeply human" and claimed that "nothing human must be foreign to the heart of the Church."[13] This emphasis on the human and on the church's accompaniment specifically in moments of suffering fleshes out more fully Romero's christologically based focus on situations of suffering and death in his own interpretation of the signs.

The church is characterized by its humanity but also by its transcendence, the second aspect that Romero emphasizes and that aids us in understanding the church's task of discerning the signs. The church's transcendence clearly cannot mean the church is somehow "above" the everyday problems of human society, given what we discussed in the previous paragraph, nor does it mean the church is immune to sin or weakness. In fact, Romero speaks to the way the church's transcendence allows it to elevate and rightly respect that which is human. In defending the church against the suspicion that it is becoming too political, Romero does so by arguing that what the church does is give human knowledge and gifts "a Christian sense." The church "brings divine value to all that is human."[14] This responsibility to all that is human includes the defense of human dignity and the image of God in human beings, especially in those whose dignity is continually trampled—that is, the poor and marginalized.

This transcendent vision that elevates all that is human includes an eschatological vision that allows the church to rightly interpret the signs of the times. The church can discern rightly the sin at work in the world in light of its understanding of God's ultimate intentions for creation. For Romero and much of the Latin American church, it was this eschatological vision that undergirded their work toward liberation. Romero articulates these theological connections:

> The eschatological sense of the Church has been illumined marvelously by the Vatican Council and also by Medellín, as an invitation to men to work on this Earth, to bring about—ever since Christ was resurrected and is now part of the history of this world—a realization of that kingdom that will be consummated in eternity.[15]

This vision thus guides both aspects of the church's interpretation of the signs that were mentioned above: (1) discerning where the Spirit is at work liberating individuals and groups in a way that corresponds to the kingdom and (2) identifying and naming sin in its own context.

If we discern in the signs of the times both where the Spirit is at work and where sin is wreaking havoc, this is in order to more fully live out the church's calling to be "the body of Christ in history."[16] The gospel is not lived out in a vacuum or in the abstract. The church does not exist apart from its social, cultural, and political context. As the body of Christ in history, the church both preaches and embodies the coming kingdom, that same kingdom Christ preached and lived out in his ministry, culminating in his death and resurrection. Romero identifies the church's embodiment of Christ's presence in history specifically as a denouncing of sin through its speech, which is inseparable from its preaching of the kingdom. Just as Christ denounced the sin of his time—the sin "of his Herods, of his Pilates, of his Pharisees"—his same voice today, via the church, denounces the abuse of power and the idolatry of money so prominent in El Salvador.[17] This aspect of the church's discernment and witness will require a *historicized* denunciation of sin that attends to both the personal and structural elements in a given society and historical moment.

Romero understood that both for the church and for individuals, turning toward God and away from evil—conversion—happens only in the concrete circumstances in which we live. Humans exist as sociopolitical creatures embedded in multiple communities with complex features. Thus, Romero could speak of conversion in his own context as being "converted to what God wants in this moment in the history of El Salvador."[18] Just as the church is the church only as it enacts the kingdom of God in its own historical context, so too any individual who converts must be converted to the particularities of God's mission in their own time and context. For Romero it was clear that what God wanted in that moment in El Salvador was a conversion to the poor and to a spirit of poverty.

But many disagreed with Romero and with the hermeneutic he used for interpreting the signs of the times, not to mention how he thought the church ought to respond to such signs. And this leads to my final point regarding the "why" of interpreting the signs of the times. Such interpretation allows the church to live as the body of Christ in history, but *discernment* and *interpretation* are required precisely because historical events are not transparent to God's purposes, and because we humans are so easily deceived by our age-old idols of power, wealth, and status.

The Christological Criterion for Interpreting the Signs of the Times

Referencing Jesus's resistance to these common idols in his desert temptations, Costadoat highlights Jesus's own words about the signs of the times (Matt 16:3) as his call to have "faith in the God who stimulates a free and creative praxis, in place of trusting in a Messiah who can impose himself on others via power and prestige."[19] Contrary to Satan's offers and to the wishes of many around him, Jesus rejects the path of power and domination. Why does Jesus chastise his hearers in Matthew 16? The Pharisees and Sadducees are asking him for a sign, and we can infer such a sign would be one that exhibited his "power and prestige," his ability to rescue his people from the rule of an oppressive empire. Just a little later in the same Gospel, after Peter has been declared "blessed" for confessing that Jesus is the Messiah, Jesus rebukes Peter for insisting that Jesus's predictions about his own suffering must not come to pass. Peter does not understand what that messianic path will entail, but Jesus does.

This discussion brings us then to the key by which we interpret the signs of the time: *a christological and cruciform key*. The church must read history through a cruciform lens and take upon itself Christlike cruciformity. Not unlike the christological hermeneutic that ought to guide our reading of Scripture, we interpret history not through the typical lens of power, dominion, and influence, but rather with the crucified Christ as our touchstone. Costadoat captures this dynamic well:

> The invocation of the expression "signs of the times" finds in the praxis of Jesus the criterion of its correct interpretation. The best of the interpretations, in harmony with the biblical texts, arises from the conviction that God, through Jesus, changes history from underneath, from the poor; from those who don't have *the* rationale to history, but rather who hope to have attained it.[20]

It is through this lens of the crucified Christ that we judge the ebbs and flows of history, knowing that those gaining power and dominance do not necessarily have God "on their side." Indeed, given the scriptural witness, they most likely do not. Through this lens we understand that the Spirit is often at work in the neglected, marginalized, and hidden places of the world. It was for this reason that Romero and other Latin American Christian leaders placed the poor at the center of their scriptural interpretation and pastoral praxis. As Romero repeatedly insisted, this was not motivated by Marxism, but by Scripture itself, under the guidance of the Spirit.

Jesus's desert temptations, his challenge to the Pharisees and Sadducees, and his rebuke of Peter—not to mention countless additional stories in all four gospels—all point in one direction: history is not transparent to God's purposes, and humans are prone to interpret history poorly, particularly when caught up by the temptations of power and money. Indeed, the death and resurrection of Jesus reinforce these lessons. In other words, interpreting the signs of the times should press us to a faith in God that serves as an *antithesis* to trusting earthly power, governments, the wealthy, militaries. Jesus instructs his followers to look beyond the "obvious" meaning of societal structures, historical events, and power relationships. Interpreting the signs of the times is by definition *not to trust* the meanings that seem most natural and common sense and certainly not trusting the interpretation that those in power give them.

White Evangelicals in the United States and Interpreting the Signs of the Times

To pray at the U.S. Congress, to preach at the White House, or to "give the blessing" at a stockholder's meeting is not political and is therefore acceptable. But to speak at a farm worker's rally, to bless their efforts to organize, and to criticize the Immigration Services is political. If one looks at the clear contradiction in such views, it is clear that the "apolitical" understanding of Christianity is very political indeed and is intended to support the agenda of the status quo. (Justo González)[21]

In *Taking America Back for God: Christian Nationalism in the United States*, sociologists Andrew Whitehead and Samuel Perry place clear research and analysis before those who care to pay attention to the relationship between Christian nationalism, white evangelical Christianity, and the state of politics in the United States.[22] Whitehead and Perry define Christian nationalism as "a cultural framework—a collection of myths, traditions, symbols, narratives, and value systems—that idealizes and advocates a fusion of Christianity with American civic life."[23] They specify further that this framework "blurs distinctions between Christian identity and American identity" and "is undergirded by identification with a conservative political orientation (though not necessarily a political party), Bible belief, premillennial visions of moral decay, and divine sanction for conquest."[24] Above all, Christian nationalism serves as a hermeneutic for interpreting the past and the important events and trends of the present. We might even say that the Christian nationalist framework shapes how many Americans "interpret the signs of the times."

Two important takeaways from Whitehead and Perry's analysis regarding the influence of Christian nationalism on white evangelicals present us simultaneously with urgency and hope. First, it comes as no surprise that a far higher percentage of white evangelicals score high on the Christian nationalism scale than other religious groups.[25] Hence, the urgency and critical nature of the problem. At the same time, Whitehead and Perry demonstrate that Christian nationalism is an entirely *separable influence* from religious affiliation and even racial identity. They demonstrate that two individuals from entirely different religious groups who both embrace Christian nationalism are "much more alike politically" than two individuals from the same religious group who score on the opposite ends of the Christian nationalism scale.[26] Furthermore, while scoring high on "religious practice" is positively associated with embracing Christian nationalism (as are many other ideological and theological factors), such a high score can also lead to a divergence in moral commitments from those of Christian nationalism. Specifically, scoring high on religious practice is positively correlated with commitments to the vulnerable, social justice, and reducing consumption for environmental reasons.[27]

I propose that Christian nationalism has become for many white evangelicals—though not for all of them, and not only for white evangelicals—a false alternative to the embodiment of the gospel that the church is called to as "the body of Christ in history." Christian nationalism in the United States is contextualized and concrete, as Christian conversion and praxis must be, but it co-opts Christian beliefs in service of a concrete *political* vision—one that is taken for granted (not questioned)—instead of allowing the Christian gospel to highlight both the good and the bad in that vision. The narratives and myths of Christian nationalism—that is, Christian nationalism's interpretation of both past and present—have been embraced for those age-old reasons humans have always worshiped at the feet of false gods: power and status. Whitehead and Perry point out that

Discerning the "Signs of the Times"

despite appearances, "the calls to 'take America back for God' are not primarily about mobilizing the faithful toward *religious* ends." Rather, the groups who espouse these views "are instead seeking to retain or gain power in the public sphere—whether political, social, or religious."[28] These narratives and myths provide the filter through which the signs of the times are interpreted, instead of the crucified Christ and the kingdom he embodied.

In seeking such power and buying into these narratives, Christians who adopt this ideology enflesh *anti-God* forces instead of incarnating the crucified Christ. Like many who opposed Jesus in his time, they read God's purposes from current events according to the human values of power and status, and assume God's blessing is with the victors of history. Those doing public theology with and for white evangelicals, as well as the pastors and leaders white evangelicals trust, must take on the task of challenging these false interpretations of the signs of our times. A first step is simply laying out the theological basis and principles for the task of interpretation, as white evangelicals tend to downplay the importance of living out the gospel in concrete circumstances. That is, white evangelicals have often presented their spirituality and their understanding of the gospel as if it existed in a vacuum, uninfluenced by culture or historical circumstances. At the same time, as sociologist Wes Markofski points out, "a large body of research suggests that evangelical practices in general...are often conditioned more by social and contextual factors than by explicitly 'religious' ones."[29] Choosing to ignore this reality is one contributing factor to the dynamic Justo González pinpoints in the quote at the beginning of this section: white Christians can label their own actions and commitments as "apolitical"—for example, lobbying against abortion—while labeling those who advocate from a faith basis for systemic changes to our immigration or economic system as "too political." Public theologians and leaders seeking to disciple white evangelicals away from Christian nationalism must begin by unmasking the ways the faith has been co-opted to serve a political vision. They must offer an alternative for embodying the faith in the concrete circumstances of the United States in the twenty-first century, with an intentional focus on interpreting the signs of our times, Christ crucified as the hermeneutical key for such interpretation.

NOTES

1. Vatican Council II, *Pastoral Constitution on the Church in the Modern World: Gaudium et Spes* (1965), 4, http://www.vatican.va/archive/hist_councils/ii_vatican_council/documents/vat-ii_const_19651207_gaudium-et-spes_en.html. Hereafter cited within the text as *GS*.

2. Albert Mohler, "The Briefing January 13, 2021," Albert Mohler, January 13, 2021, https://albertmohler.com/2021/01/13/briefing-1-13-21.

3. As quoted in Molly Olmstead, "'Christian Nationalism' Used to Be Taboo. Now It's All the Rage," *Slate*, August 5, 2022, https://slate.com/news-and-politics/2022/08/christian-nationalist-identity-marjorie-taylor-greene.html.

4. Mons. Óscar Arnulfo Romero, "La dimension política de la fe desde la opción por los pobres," in *Cartas Pastorales y Discursos de Monseñor Oscar A. Romero*, ed. Centro Monseñor Romero (San Salvador: UCA, 2007), 187. Translation mine, here and throughout, unless otherwise indicated.

5. John XXIII, *Humanae Salutis* (1961), https://www.vatican.va/content/john-xxiii/es/apost_constitutions/1961/documents/hf_j-xxiii_apc_19611225_humanae-salutis.html.

6. Eduardo Pironio, "Interpretación Cristiana de los Signos de los Tiempos Hoy en América Latina," *Medellín: Teología y Pastoral para América Latina* 44, no. 171 (2018): 80. Fundación Dialnet.

7. Pironio, "Interpretación Cristiana de los Signos de los Tiempos," 81.

8. Jorge Costadoat, "Teología de los Signos de los Tiempos, un Itinerario Latinamericano," *Revista Latinoamerican de Teología* 110 (2020): 177. Fundación Dialnet.

9. Donal Dorr, "The Perspective of the Poor: What We Can Learn from Liberation Theology about the 'Signs of the Times,'" in *Scrutinizing the Signs of the Times in the Light of the Gospel*, ed. Johan Verstraeten (Leuven: University Press, 2007), 247.

10. Dorr, "The Perspective of the Poor," 248.

11. Mons. Óscar Arnulfo Romero, "La historia de la salvación" (Aug. 7, 1977), in *Homilías*, vol. 1 (San Salvador: UCA Editores, 2006), 240.

12. Mons. Óscar Arnulfo Romero, "Un Juicio de Dios" (Nov. 19, 1978), in *Homilías*, vol. 3 (San Salvador: UCA Editores, 2006), 441.

13. Romero, "Un Juicio de Dios," 441.

14. Romero, "La Iglesia Misionera" (Oct. 23, 1977), in *Homilías*, 1:416.

15. Romero, "Características de nuestra Iglesia" (Aug. 21, 1977), in *Homilías*, 1:276.

16. This was the title of his second pastoral letter, dated Aug. 6, 1977. Óscar Romero, *La Iglesia, cuerpo de Cristo en la historia: Segunda carta pastoral* (San Salvador, 1977).

17. Romero, "La Iglesia de la alianza de Dios y de la verdadera pobreza" (Aug. 28, 1977), in *Homilías*, 1:286.

18. Romero, "Características de nuestra Iglesia" (Aug. 21, 1977), in *Homilías*, 1:278.

19. Costadoat, "Teología de los Signos de los Tiempos," 169.

20. Costadoat, "Teología de los signos de los tiempos," 170. Emphasis original.

21. Justo Gonzalez, *Mañana: Christian Theology from a Hispanic Perspective* (Nashville: Abingdon Press, 1990), 84.

22. Andrew Whitehead and Samuel Perry, *Taking America Back for God: Christian Nationalism in the United States* (New York: Oxford University Press, 2020).

23. Whitehead and Perry, *Taking America Back for God*, 10.

24. Whitehead and Perry, *Taking America Back for God*, 15.

25. Whitehead and Perry, *Taking America Back for God*, 30.

26. Whitehead and Perry, *Taking America Back for God*, 153.

27. Whitehead and Perry, *Taking America Back for God*, 15.

28. Whitehead and Perry, *Taking America Back for God*, 153. Emphasis original.

29. Wes Markofski, "Reflexive Evangelicalism," *Political Power and Social Theory* 36 (2019): 53.

10

THE RELIGIOUS SIGNIFICANCE OF ANOREXIA

Caroline Morris

I once interviewed for a job at an eating disorder clinic, and the moment I walked in, I tensed and thought, "I would never get well here." It was no different from your typical professional setting: clean, organized, and controlled. The three or four receptionists who greeted me weren't just dressed in immaculate business attire; they were also slim and fit, glowing pictures of perfect health. The underlying assumption, stated explicitly midinterview, was that what the recovering anorexic needs is an example, someone who follows all the rules, someone to model healthy eating and living for them.

I went to a conference on eating disorders several months later, out of both personal and professional interest, and had the same experience. It wasn't just the raw vegetables and salad they served me over the course of the day or the unfortunate conversations I overheard during lunch—there was an overall atmosphere of virtue and cleanliness, of imagined health, that I found deeply disturbing. It was particularly disturbing in light of my studies on the matter, through which I discovered that a great deal of research backs up what I already knew experientially: anorexia is an ascetic disorder, where virtue rather than beauty is at stake.[1]

The Religious Significance of Anorexia

While there is nothing wrong with raw vegetables or salad, there is nothing *right* with them either, and watching a hundred or so people exclusively eating "clean," low-calorie foods while wearing Diet Culture Dropout tees was quite a sight. My partner's favorite saying, which amusingly communicates both a great deal and almost nothing, comes to mind: "There is something to be said about this." The conversations I overheard varied in subject and offensiveness, but most unfortunate in my estimation were the stories the students and clinicians told each other about their clients with anorexia. They were venting, which I suppose they had every right to do at a conference with their peers, but the feelings of disdain and superiority they communicated were personally offensive, generally concerning, and interesting all at once.

It seemed to me that my tablemates had misunderstood or forgotten something essential about anorexia, what drives it and what resolves it. Simona Giordano, professor of bioethics, asserts at the end of *Understanding Eating Disorders* that the way to resolve what we call eating disorders is to challenge "the way we—*all of us*—think about concepts such as right and wrong, good, and bad" and the way we feel compelled to moralize everything.[2] I expected those I met at this conference to be doing the hard work of challenging the ways that eating and health are so pervasively moralized, but I left feeling disappointed. While I will begin this chapter by recasting anorexia as an ascetic disorder and emphasizing its mechanistic simplicity, I will also suggest that it is contextual and that we are all complicit to varying degrees in its development.

In the last few decades, several eating-disorder researchers have observed that what they are dealing with when they deal with anorexia—a loose category, with permeable boundaries—is morality. While the general public's conception of anorexia tends to be that it is a disease in which people, affluent Western women primarily, are "dieting madly for appearance," this way of thinking "does not adequately explain cases on either side of the globe."[3] Research done by sociologist Catherine Garrett, social anthropologist Megan Warin, psychiatrist Sing Lee, and others challenges not only the concept of anorexia as being inextricably linked to any particular culture but also the "beauty explanation" and the claim that "fat phobia" is an "essential clinical feature of anorexia."[4] Even when fat is feared and thinness is sought, thinness, Giordano reminds us, "is not simply a matter of what we find *pretty*. It is a matter of what we believe to be *good and right*."[5] Anthropologists Richard O'Connor and Penny Van Esterik likewise found that the connection between fat phobia and anorexia was overhyped. In their interviews with those who know anorexia experientially, they found not "adolescent girls literally dying for looks" but "youthful ascetics" concerned primarily with virtue.[6]

While today's anorexic is not necessarily religious, there seems to be both a moral and religious energy to anorexia.[7] Medical anthropologist Caroline Giles Banks encourages researchers to pay close attention to the anorexic's connection to and experience of religion,[8] because, in doing just that, she found that religious beliefs continue to play a role in some women's subjective experience of their anorexia.[9] Banks attributes this finding to the continuing presence of ascetic ideals, especially those related to food and sex, within Christian traditions.[10] With a focus on experiences of recovery, Catherine Garrett shares that many of her interviewees realized that their recovery was dependent upon the "'spiritual' discourses available to them."[11] These participants referred to their anorexia as a sort of spiritual pilgrimage—a long and dangerous journey away from a distorted spirituality and toward a healthy, whole one that centers connection with the self, with others, and with the world. "If we listen carefully," Mary Michelle Lelwica, professor of religious and gender studies and author of *Starving for Salvation*, writes, we will find that stories of anorexia are "multifaceted, diverse, and permeated with symbolic and ritual—one might argue, religious—significance."[12]

Listening carefully to the anorexic's account of their own story is essential in understanding the conception and development of anorexia as well as the way out of it. However, there is a tension to hold when talking about what we call anorexia nervosa: there is meaning to be found in it, even made from it, and it is also meaningless. While there are many meaning-imbued gateways to anorexia and perhaps even more ways to make meaning of it, anorexia is, at its core, really rather simple and even mechanical.[13] The pieces of each person's story can be both understood and arranged in meaningful ways, yet the only reasonable cause of anorexia is the single unifying trait in all cases across time: "the activity of starving."[14] Before diving into the gateways to anorexia relevant to Christianity, it is important to understand "the internal gravity that makes the disease."[15]

The Religious Significance of Anorexia

While anyone, regardless of age, gender, cultural background, and the like, can develop anorexia, it seems to occur most often in adolescence. Psychiatrist S. Louis Mogul proposes asceticism as the link between adolescence and anorexia. Mogul suggests that anorexia happens when the adolescent reaches "for normal adolescent attitudes" in order to defend against the rush of their libidinal demands, of their instinctual desires, but these attitudes are "taken to absurd extremes."[16] What was to be an aid in their natural quest to exercise control over the libido ends up crushing the libido, so that the only "trace of libidinal pleasure" in some cases is "a joyless masochism."[17] Mogul writes that the difference between normal and dangerous asceticism is "not so much its extent, or even the subjective experience of gratification from it, but the degree to which the asceticism becomes an end in itself."[18] This is precisely what happens within the individual who develops anorexia: the asceticism that has been so resourcefully, or accidentally, taken up becomes an end in itself.

In *The Ego and the Mechanisms of Defense*, psychoanalyst Anna Freud—daughter of Sigmund Freud—likens the asceticism of adolescents to "the asceticism of religious fanatics,"[19] and writes that such self-denial can be seen as a "manifestation of the innate hostility between the ego and the instincts."[20] Freud writes that when "the ego in some inexplicable way is strong enough to carry through its repudiation of instinct without any deviation," the adolescent falls into "a kind of catatonic condition."[21] Further, and more of the essence, Freud writes, "This adolescent mistrust of instinct has a dangerous tendency to spread; it may begin with instinctual wishes proper and extend to the most ordinary physical needs"—which is, of course, where anorexia comes in.[22] Like Freud, O'Connor and Van Esterik note the similarity between the anorexic and the religious ascetic. They share that their interviewees reported "the same transcendent high of purity and bodily mastery that religious ascetics celebrate."[23] The anorexic, like the ascetic, "chooses and keeps a regimen that denies creature comforts," and it is this choice that is the common denominator in all cases of confirmed or perceived anorexia nervosa across history.[24] The behavior of the anorexic-to-be, intentional or not, activates a mechanism, and anorexia happens.

Despite this actual simplicity, it is evident that those who do develop anorexia often do so by simply following cultural rules. O'Connor and Van Esterik point out that their interviewees seem to be echoing "how contemporary culture moralizes eating,"[25] and Giordano writes that eating disorders consist "of ordinary morality, which is just being *taken seriously*."[26] The anorexic's logic, Giordano explains, is a *"moral logic."*[27] Others, like Megan Warin, assert similarly that people with anorexia are simply following their culture's rules of hygiene in order to "cleanse themselves and their environments."[28] The participants in Warin's study "used hygienic practices to disconnect themselves from...foods, bodily processes, memories, experiences, and emotions."[29] These practices are "hidden in the persuasions of cultural logic."[30] All four of these researchers look at the person with anorexia in context rather than within a framework of individual pathology, and when the anorexic is seen in context, it becomes clear that their actions make sense.

In *Holy Anorexia*, historian Rudolph Bell explores the relationship between contemporary anorexia as he understands it—some of his descriptions are outdated and insulting—and the asceticism of the female saint. Bell writes that the so-called holy anorexics were unable to return to the table because, for them, the goal of fasting was never complete. There is a distinction to be made between the behavior of those who fasted imitating Jesus in the wilderness, for a set period and for a clear purpose, and this particularly female experience. These women reportedly claimed that they were unable to eat, even when they were ordered to do so by their superiors, because they *"believed their bodies could not be purified and actively sought to destroy them."*[31] As Warin's research shows, the modern anorexic is likewise concerned with purity and cleanliness, often viewing their restrictive behaviors around eating as cleansing rituals meant to counter "abjection."[32] These cleansing rituals go beyond the realm of food restriction, for anorexia does not only involve a disconnection from food and eating but from anything of the body—all bodily functions and appetites are experienced as "disgusting and out of place."[33] At the heart of anorexia is the desire "to be empty, pure, and clean."[34]

That the modern anorexic is, like the medieval ascetic, concerned primarily with virtue is something O'Connor and Van Esterik are adamant that "simple observation" could have explained.[35] They cite sociologist Julius H. Rubin's study of "religious melancholy" and state, "Four centuries ago English physicians could explain what now mystifies us. By *observing* their patients *in context* they realized anorexia came from leading an overly pious life."[36] In his book,

The Religious Significance of Anorexia

Rubin writes of the "evangelical anorexic,"[37] a religious person who was "obsessed with personal rituals of purification" because they were painfully convinced that they were beyond God's forgiveness.[38] This is reminiscent of the fasting saints Bell and others describe and, stripped of the God language, it sounds a lot like the experience of contemporary women with anorexia. Although what Rubin refers to as evangelical anorexia is in a sense bound to a particular culture, just as Rudolph Bell's "holy anorexia"—characterized by a "need to establish a sense of oneself, a contest of wills, a quest for autonomy"[39] or, as medievalist Caroline Walker Bynum described it, the inability to eat anything other than the "eucharistic host"[40]—is bound to monastic culture in Medieval Europe, the *essence* of anorexia is not so bound. It is not even bound to religion, though Banks shows that some form of evangelical or fundamentalist-religious anorexia still exists.[41]

O'Connor and Van Esterik point out that today's anorexic lacks a religious tradition "to rein in excess,"[42] to condemn and correct overly pious behavior. On the matter of reining in ascetic excess, Rubin cites Robert Burton, a seventeenth-century religious scholar, who writes of the affliction that proceeds from "too much fasting, meditation, precise life" and advises the person so afflicted to "ease the soul by all honest recreations, refresh and recreate [their] distressed soul."[43] Burton, in the seventeenth century, is able to see what O'Connor and Van Esterik see, that ascetic excess is the problem and must be countered with actual excess. Like Burton, Freud writes that when the prohibitions she describes are followed by a period of excess, in which the adolescent begins to partake of all that they had previously denied themselves, there is hope. Though such excesses may not appear to be and may not be good per se, they "represent transitory spontaneous recovery from the condition of asceticism."[44]

If anorexia is indeed an ascetic disorder, then both one single and many possible causes for it exist. While the theory we are working with here is that starvation itself turns a person into a starver,[45] the way that any culture understands gender may affect who is more likely to develop the condition. Within Christianity, women, in a different way than men, have been affected by teachings about purifying and controlling the body, "for women generally carry the greater burden of human fleshliness."[46] It is women who have been told most consistently that their drives are evil. It is women who have been trained in renunciation, and as Sandra M. Gilbert and Susan

Gubar write in *Madwoman in the Attic*, "To be trained in renunciation is almost necessarily to be trained to ill health, since the human animal's first and strongest urge is to his/her *own* survival, pleasure, assertion."[47] They offer the example of the nineteenth-century ideal of "beautiful and 'frail'" femininity and how this ideal "led to tight-lacing and vinegar-drinking."[48] There are a number of researchers who take this view—the view that, in exhibiting anorexic behaviors, women are "simply [carrying] patriarchal definitions of 'femininity' to absurd extremes."[49] While this answer cannot be *the answer*, it is possible that women are more likely to develop anorexia because they are more likely to be encouraged to develop and maintain the practices that trigger anorexia.[50]

Regulation of the female appetite can be traced back to the Genesis story of how the world began and was subsequently infected, temporarily ruined: "In the Genesis narrative of the fall, sin and death enter the world when a woman eats."[51] The story of the fall is a prime example of what philosopher Helene Cixous calls "libidinal education."[52] The term *libidinal* refers here to all "bodily and sexual experience"[53] and to all basic appetites—whether for food, sex, knowledge, or power. The accompanying term, *libidinal education*, refers to "the individual's discovery of the body and the cultural prohibitions surrounding it."[54] In her essay on "Hunger" in *Feminist Perspectives on Eating Disorders*, Naomi Wolf discusses the ways that women and girls have been taught to deny their hunger, to stifle their appetites. She ends her essay with a description of how a young girl might experience life if she, like her male peers, were encouraged to eat her fill. She asks rhetorically, "Who knows what she would do? Who knows what it would feel like?"[55] The answer, of course, is that few have experienced even a glimmer of the freedom Wolf describes; it requires unlearning and retraining. When a woman eats her fill or eats as she pleases, she is rebelling, retraining herself to strive after her own "survival, pleasure, and assertion."[56]

Because Christian teachings have for some played a role in the problem by opening gateways to the disorder, traditional religion can play a role in recovery. One way to do this is through reinterpretation. The story of Eve, reread, offers an exploration of a new kind of libidinal education that fosters appreciation for the existence, expression, and fulfillment of desire. In Cixous's interpretation of the Genesis story, Eve's consumption of the apple is seen as a "paradigmatic moment of female rebellion against the invisible and negative force of patriarchal law."[57] In the ancient story, Eve discovers herself, her body, and the whole world through her mouth, showing that "knowledge and taste go together."[58] In exchange for tasting knowledge, Eve must pay a price, and this story functions as a warning for all women. To Naomi Wolf's question of what would happen if a young girl—or if any woman—ate as she pleased, Cixous answers, she would *know*, she would discover the "inside," and she, like Eve, would be punished.

In *Reinventing Eve*, author and counselor Kim Chernin offers a reading of the Genesis creation account in which she seeks to "discover and believe Eve's version of the Eden story."[59] The dominant reading of the story turns every woman into "an Eve, indicted as the cause of evil and the corrupter of men and angels."[60] This was likely both intentional and practical; the authors wanted to explain evil and to do it in such a way that "the cultural facts of male dominance and female subservience" were justified.[61] The story, "as it has been interpreted by male religious leaders," "discredits, devalues, and redefines symbols of prepatriarchal cultures."[62] Chernin, in looking at Eve's side of the story, revisits the symbols of prepatriarchal cultures and portrays the serpent as a positive character, rather than a cunning tempter. As for Eve, and thus all who possess her nature, she is no longer "the gateway of the Devil," as Tertullian supposed,[63] nor is she inherently "defective and misbegotten" as Thomas Aquinas alleged.[64] That is one version of the story, but Chernin tells it differently.

Chernin's Eve did not sin when she broke the Male Creator's rule and ate, though it was certainly an act of defiance. Eve succumbed to temptation, but this temptation came to her from the benevolent whisper of a serpent that desired to free her, by reminding her "of the primal and visceral knowledge: to be female is not to be weak, but rather to be strong; not to be seductive, but rather to be re-source-full (filled as the Source of birth and of being)."[65] In eating the fruit, Eve also tasted knowledge, a specific kind of knowledge: "that female creative power all mention of which has been left out of the Genesis story, except for the obscure symbol of the fruit tree."[66] Chernin points out that this fruit tree belongs, in other ancient traditions, to a goddess,[67] and she suggests that the tree was there not because God put it there but because it belonged there, representing femininity in an otherwise masculine narrative.[68] And so, it becomes possible to "reinvent" Eve, to reimagine the meaning of the whole story. It was not vice but virtue within Eve that prompted her to consume the "apple of possibility."[69] I recall Naomi Wolf's question: *Who knows what it would feel like?*[70] This is the possibility that Eve consumes, the world of possibilities she opens up with her glorious, defiant act.

Thanks to Eve, there is hope for what Chernin calls the "Woman Who Is Not Yet."[71] Eve, in this reading, opens the possibility of women making sense of themselves. Rather than serving as a warning to women to stay inside the lines drawn for them—or else—the story of Eve can have another purpose. It can be an aid when women find themselves facing the same decision Eve faced, as all have and do and will again, a decision: "Between renunciation and appetite...subordination and desire...submission and power...hunger as temptation and hunger as vision."[72] It can encourage women to seek the knowledge that will finally allow them to make themselves in an image they recognize, into themselves, whatever that ends up looking like.

This reinvention of the story of Eve is empowering for all women: "To imagine Eve, the sinful first woman, as rebel in Paradise, is itself a bite into the forbidden fruit."[73] But it may be powerful in a unique way to women struggling with eating disorders. Theologian Mary Louise Bringle, who shares her own experiences with bulimia in *The God of Thinness*, writes of the effect Chernin's reading of the story had on her: "In its affirmation of food and fecundity and femaleness and the flesh, it *gives me back my appetite.*"[74] It would seem that misogynistic religious traditions *sometimes* play a role in the entry to the disorder, as they encourage women to develop appetite-denying practices, and O'Connor and Van Esterik show that the essence of anorexia is "hidden in plain sight"—within the anorexic's practices.[75] Traditional, patriarchal readings of the text take away the notion of appetite as life giving, condemning as they do "food and fecundity and femaleness and the flesh,"[76] and these alternative readings[77] have the ability to give women back what was taken from them: a healthy appetite, the expression of which is in their control.

Bringle's only corrective to Chernin's reinvention of Eve is the point that "some tasting *is* dangerous," and the sort of tasting that might be deemed "dangerous," she says, is that which requires her to "take eagerly from another with thought only for myself."[78] This is fair, yet it also seems unnecessary. Of course an unrestrained appetite that exploits or harms others is wrong, but most women do not need to hear that message. That would be akin to telling "the Angel in

The Religious Significance of Anorexia

the House"—the self-effacing, self-forgetful, others-oriented housewife—to take care not to be selfish. It is a balanced view, but what is needed is more revolutionary. Those who have been oppressed and objectified need time to revel in their subjectivity, in the beauty of their selves, including, even, the fulfillment of their "selfish" desires. Eating, drinking, playing, dreaming, exploring one's sexuality—these are all life-affirming ways to combat asceticism.

Garrett's research on "the creation of the non-anorexic self" is analogous in some ways to Chernin's woman-who-is-not-yet. Both see recovery as involving a reconnection with desire, hunger, and pleasure, and Garrett found that "the metaphorical relation between unsatisfied hunger for understanding, terror in the face of sexuality and the denial of pleasure in food" were important themes in her participants' stories.[79] That these three appetites—for knowledge, sexuality, and food—are themes in the stories of present and former anorexics is interesting, considering Freud's assertion of the importance of excess in the adolescents' recovery from asceticism. Excesses of libidinal fulfillment, however "unwelcome" such excesses may be, are representative of recovery.[80] Garrett seconds this, writing, "The re-awakening or recognition of desire (for food, for sexual experience, for nature, and for life itself) is essential to the ongoing creation of the new 'non-anorexic' self. Desire is inseparable from spirituality, since both are the life-force which animates existence."[81] If fasting can be seen as an attempt "to confront the essentially spiritual problem of one's own existence,"[82] then recovery has to do with reanimating existence, through the acceptance, recognition, and fulfillment of desire.

Like the woman who interviewed me years ago at an eating disorder clinic, I understand that having an example can be an important part of the recovery process. However, in light of the connection between anorexia and virtue, I posit that it would be most useful for the recovering anorexic to watch and emulate those who are *not* following the rules: those concerned only with the life-affirming nature of eating; those open to pleasure, cravings, and fulfillment. In the latter half of my own recovery journey, I was drawn in various ways to people whose behaviors and ways of being affirmed "a world in which touching and tasting are good."[83] Observing these embodied affirmations slowly gave me back my appetite, for touching and tasting, thinking and writing, for life itself. What I learned from my encounters with both this clinic and this conference, aside from the sudden awareness that those spaces were not good for me, was that Giordano was right about the solution—it involves all of us. Clinics and conferences, Christian churches and communities, we all need to reflect on the ways that we enforce "the rules," whatever they happen to be.

NOTES

1. Richard A. O'Connor and Penny Van Esterik, "De-medicalizing Anorexia: A New Cultural Brokering," *Anthropology Today* 24, no. 5 (2008): 8.

2. Simona Giordano, *Understanding Eating Disorders: Conceptual and Ethical Issues in the Treatment of Anorexia and Bulimia Nervosa* (New York: Oxford University Press, 2005), 264.

3. O'Connor and Van Esterik, "De-medicalizing Anorexia," 6.

4. Catherine J. Garrett, *Beyond Anorexia: Narrative, Spirituality, and Recovery* (Cambridge: Cambridge University Press, 1998); Megan Warin, *Studies in Medical Anthropology: Abject Relations; Everyday Worlds of Anorexia* (New Brunswick, NJ: Rutgers University Press, 2009); Sing Lee, "Self-Starvation in Context: Towards a Culturally Sensitive Understanding of Anorexia Nervosa," *Social Science & Medicine* 41, no. 1 (1995): 25–36.

5. Giordano, *Understanding Eating Disorders*, 104.

6. O'Connor and Van Esterik, "De-medicalizing Anorexia," 6.

7. Richard A. O'Connor and Penny Van Esterik, *From Virtue to Vice: Negotiating Anorexia* (New York: Berghahn Books, 2015), 25.

8. P. Scott Richards, Randy K. Hardman, and Michael E. Berrett, *Spiritual Approaches in the Treatment of Women with Eating Disorders* (Washington, DC: American Psychological Association, 2007), 26.

9. Caroline Giles Banks, "There Is No Fat in Heaven," *Gastronomica: The Journal of Food and Culture* 3, no. 4 (2003): 124.

10. Banks, "There Is No Fat in Heaven," 126.

11. Catherine J. Garrett, "Recovery from Anorexia: A Durkheimian Interpretation," *Social Science & Medicine* 43, no. 10 (1996): 1491.

12. Michelle Mary Lelwica, *Starving for Salvation* (New York: Oxford University Press, 1999), 29.

13. O'Connor and Van Esterik, *From Virtue to Vice*, 9.

14. O'Connor and Van Esterik, *From Virtue to Vice*, 114.
15. O'Connor and Van Esterik, *From Virtue to Vice*, 9.
16. S. L. Mogul, "Asceticism in Adolescence and Anorexia Nervosa," *The Psychoanalytic Study of the Child* 35 (1980): 6.
17. Mogul, "Asceticism in Adolescence and Anorexia Nervosa," 14.
18. Mogul, "Asceticism in Adolescence and Anorexia Nervosa," 4.
19. Anna Freud, *The Ego and the Mechanisms of Defense* (London: Hogarth Press, 1937), 167.
20. Freud, *The Ego and the Mechanisms of Defense*, 172.
21. Freud, *The Ego and the Mechanisms of Defense*, 170.
22. Freud, *The Ego and the Mechanisms of Defense*, 168.
23. O'Connor and Van Esterik, *From Virtue to Vice*, 24.
24. O'Connor and Van Esterik, *From Virtue to Vice*, 24.
25. O'Connor and Van Esterik, "De-medicalizing Anorexia," 7–8.
26. Giordano, *Understanding Eating Disorders*, 257.
27. Giordano, *Understanding Eating Disorders*, 257.
28. Warin, *Everyday Worlds of Anorexia*, 186.
29. Warin, *Everyday Worlds of Anorexia*, 171.
30. Warin, *Everyday Worlds of Anorexia*, 156.
31. Rudolph M. Bell, *Holy Anorexia* (Chicago: University of Chicago Press, 1987), 117–18. Emphasis added.
32. Warin, *Everyday Worlds of Anorexia*, 153.
33. Warin, *Everyday Worlds of Anorexia*, 171.
34. Warin, *Everyday Worlds of Anorexia*, 164.
35. O'Connor and Van Esterik, *From Virtue to Vice*, 117.
36. O'Connor and Van Esterik, *From Virtue to Vice*, 117
37. Julius H. Rubin, *Religious Melancholy and Protestant Experience in America* (New York: Oxford University Press, 1994), 83.
38. Rubin, *Religious Melancholy and Protestant Experience in America*, 82.
39. Bell, *Holy Anorexia*, 8.
40. Caroline Walker Bynum, *Fragmentation and Redemption: Essays on Gender and the Human Body in Medieval Religion* (New York: Zone Books, 1991), 189.

41. Caroline Giles Banks, "'Culture' in Culture-Bound Syndromes: The Case of Anorexia Nervosa," *Social Science & Medicine* 34, no. 8 (1992): 869; Banks, "There Is No Fat in Heaven."

42. O'Connor and Van Esterik, "De-medicalizing Anorexia," 6.

43. Robert Burton, *The Anatomy of Melancholy*, ed. Floyd Dell and Paul Jordan-Smith (New York: Farrar and Rinehart, 1927), 970.

44. Freud, *The Ego and the Mechanisms of Defense*, 170.

45. O'Connor and Van Esterik, *From Virtue to Vice*, 6.

46. Karen McCarthy Brown, "Fundamentalism and the Control of Women," in *Fundamentalism and Gender*, ed. John Stratton Hawley (New York: Oxford University Press, 1994), 176.

47. Sandra M. Gilbert and Susan Gubar, *Madwoman in the Attic: The Woman Writer and the Nineteenth-Century Literary Imagination* (New Haven, CT: Yale University Press, 1980), 54.

48. Gilbert and Gubar, *Madwoman in the Attic*.

49. Gilbert and Gubar, *Madwoman in the Attic*. See also Kim Chernin, *The Hungry Self: Women, Eating and Identity* (New York: Times Books, 1985); Patricia Fallon, Melanie A. Katzman, and Susan C. Wooley, eds., *Feminist Perspectives on Eating Disorders* (New York: Guilford Press, 1994); Susan Bordo, *Unbearable Weight: Feminism, Western Culture, and the Body* (Berkeley: University of California Press, 2004).

50. O'Connor and Van Esterik, *From Virtue to Vice*, 9.

51. Tamar Heller and Patricia Moran, "Introduction: Scenes of the Apple: Appetite, Desire, Writing," in *Scenes of the Apple: Food and the Female Body in Nineteenth- and Twentieth-Century Women's Writing*, ed. Tamar Heller (Albany: State University of New York Press, 2003), 1.

52. Helene Cixous, "Extreme Fidelity," in *Helene Cixous Reader*, ed. Susan Sellers (London: Routledge, 1994), 132–133.

53. Heller and Moran, "Introduction: Scenes of the Apple," 2.

54. Heller and Moran, "Introduction: Scenes of the Apple," 1.

55. Naomi Wolf, "Hunger," in *Feminist Perspectives on Eating Disorders*, ed. Patricia Fallon, Melanie A. Katzman, and Susan C. Wooley (New York: The Guilford Press, 1994), 110.

56. Gilbert and Gubar, *Madwoman in the Attic*, 54.

57. Heller and Moran, "Introduction: Scenes of the Apple," 5.

58. Cixous, "Extreme Fidelity," 132–33.

59. Kim Chernin, *Reinventing Eve: Modern Woman in Search of Herself* (New York: Times Books, 1987), 149.

60. Bernard P. Prusak, "Woman: Seductive Siren and Source of Sin?," in *Religion and Sexism: Images of Women in the Jewish and Christian Traditions*, ed. Rosemary Radford Ruether (New York: Simon and Schuster, 1974), 97.

61. Prusak, "Woman: Seductive Siren and Source of Sin?," 97.

62. O. Wayne Wooley, "...And Man Created 'Woman': Representations," in Fallon, Katzman, and Wooley, *Feminist Perspectives on Eating Disorders*, 29.

63. Alcuin Blamires, Karen Pratt, and C. William Marx, *Woman Defamed and Woman Defended: An Anthology of Medieval Texts* (New York: Clarendon Press; Oxford University Press, 1992), 51.

64. Chernin, *Reinventing Eve*, 150–51.

65. Mary Louise Bringle, *The God of Thinness: Gluttony and Other Weighty Matters* (Nashville: Abingdon Press, 1992), 88.

66. Chernin, *Reinventing Eve*, xix.

67. Chernin, *Reinventing Eve*, xvii.

68. Chernin, *Reinventing Eve*, 174.

69. Chernin, *Reinventing Eve*, xix.

70. Wolf, "Hunger," 110.

71. Chernin, *Reinventing Eve*, 120, xvii.

72. Chernin, *Reinventing Eve*, 181–82.

73. Chernin, *Reinventing Eve*, 149.

74. Bringle, *The God of Thinness*, 89.

75. O'Connor and Van Esterik, *From Virtue to Vice*, 24.

76. Bringle, *The God of Thinness*, 89.

77. See, for example, Marija Gimbutas, *The Language of the Goddess* (London: Thames & Hudson, 1989); Gerda Lerner, *The Creation of Patriarchy* (New York: Oxford University Press, 1986).

78. Bringle, *The God of Thinness*, 89.

79. Catherine J. Garrett, "Remaking the Self through Metaphor: Recovery from Anorexia Nervosa," *Health Sociology Review* 6 (1996): 152.

80. Freud, *The Ego and the Mechanisms of Defense*, 170.

81. Garrett, "Remaking the Self," 147.

82. Garrett, "Remaking the Self," 152.

83. Bringle, *The God of Thinness*, 89.

11

"TWO STRIKES"

Or Why I Write for *Women in Theology*

Jane Barter

Over twenty years ago, my ex-husband landed a job at a decidedly modern prairie university. I was still working on my PhD and had one baby in tow and another on the way. When I applied for adjunct teaching, the chair of the Religious Studies department offered these encouraging words: "*Well, you have two strikes against you—one is that you are a theologian, and the other is that you are a feminist.*" I don't know what the third strike was (perhaps it was all those pregnancy hormones I exuded), but at that university, I was forever out.

The sting of that moment still lingers as I recall it, but I suspect that when the resurrection comes, that wound will be transformed into a badge of honor, and why shouldn't it? What could be more badass than being a feminist theologian, particularly in a world in which God is *so* over, and feminism remains a source of derision and disdain? In this essay, I wish to look at the process by which theology had become sufficiently marginalized in Canada that it could be counted as a strike by beginning with some personal reflections on my own thirty-year engagement with academic theology. I also wish to look at the ways in which feminist theory is surprisingly aligned with and complementary to theology as a discipline. Finally, I wish to make a case for the urgency of both feminism and theology within the contemporary university and thus point to the significance of *Women in Theology* as a source and example of what Sara Ahmed has called "sweaty concepts."[1]

Strike One: Theology

In 1991, as I took my first classes at the Atlantic School of Theology (AST), I could hardly be faulted for not foreseeing the demise of my chosen field. The 1980s and '90s were a period of profound economic hardship in the Maritimes. This was a result of the combined forces of recession, loss of industry such as coal and steel, the moratorium on the cod fishery, and new neoliberal policies aimed at decentralization that put an end to equalization payments from richer to poorer provinces in Canada.[2] The president of AST once wryly quipped that seminary enrollments tend to soar when economic fortunes trend downward. The Maritimes had not yet seen an explosion of immigration by the early 1990s, even though the rest of Canada was beginning to see the results of Canada's immigration waves in the 1970s and '80s.[3] Because universities in Canada receive most of their funding through public grants, they are especially susceptible to the vagaries of national and provincial policy. After a brief revival of church affiliation in Canada post–Second World War, membership declined dramatically in the latter half of the twentieth century. Further, Canada responded to the growing demands of industrial and extractive capitalism by opening its doors to an unprecedented number of immigrants, which would have the effect of transforming the landscape of Canadian religious life dramatically. In 1961, 96 percent of Canadians identified as Christian; by 2011, that number declined to 67 percent.[4]

As a result of these social and political changes within Canada, religious studies departments quietly superseded theology—the latter came to represent an uncomfortable and tetchy remnant from the colonial past, like high tea, but with fewer enthusiasts. And although most universities in Canada were founded by the Catholic Church and Protestant mainline denominations (namely, the Anglican Church, the Evangelical Lutheran Church in Canada, and the United Church of Canada),[5] those denominational ties became an increasingly dim memory. In his recent book *From Seminary to University: An Institutional History of the Study of Religion in Canada*, Aaron Hughes summarizes this transition in Canadian religious education and the shift in values attendant upon it:

> Federal legislation on multiculturalism, for example, demanded that the beliefs, customs, and religions of others be taken seriously. This meant that a journal that focused narrowly on Christianity would not, for example, be eligible for federal financial support. The articulation and defence of Christian truth-claims was coming to be seen as "anachronistic and inadequate" when it came to addressing the changing ethnic and religious make-up of Canada. This is not to say that Christian theological institutions ceased to exist. It does mean, however, that they became…increasingly irrelevant for the majority of Canadians.[6]

Theology as a discipline was ill-prepared within this context to defend itself against such charges without seeming conservative and reactionary. It had three options as a result of these sea changes within Canadian public life: it could strive for independence and become a seminary or independent theological school divested from the universities that had become ambivalent about them; it could retain a degree of independence within the universities, a living relic and often in ambivalent relationship to the modern religious studies programs that sprang up beside it; or it could close its doors. The third option tended to be less a choice than an inevitability as churches in Canada continued to face steep decline.

For those schools that remained, theology was under increased pressure to justify its continued existence. It tended to do so in Canada by foregrounding professionalization and underplaying its academic vocation, thus ensuring it would not be viewed as a competitor to the new departments of religious studies. In seeing itself as a professional school, it became further distanced from programs in the liberal arts, and in undergraduate teaching, while it also became exposed to the vagaries of a declining labor market for ordained clergy.

Hughes's account of this transition is unsurprising from a religious studies scholar, who, like the chair in my pregnant encounter,

"Two Strikes"

regarded the transition from theology as an unambiguous scholarly and moral victory "from religious exclusion to secularism, from Christocentrism to culturalism, and from theology to religious studies."[7] We might pause, however, to question whether multicultural Canada and its state-sponsored universities represent a wholesale moral and intellectual victory over religious communities' own forms of knowledge.[8] In this, I am cognizant of the limitation of the term *theology* in Western forms of scholarship. The term, as I am using it, however, involves religiously situated knowledge of the subject matter that is religious phenomena, or, as Anselm described it simply as, "faith seeking understanding." The term can therefore apply (albeit with some tension) to non-Western forms of self-involving religious knowledge. The marginalization of theology and the production of knowledge by scholars of religion alone, therefore, not only affected theology, but profoundly shaped the expression of religious knowledge of new Canadians and for the First Peoples of this land for whom the distinction between religious and secular, or the superiority of the latter, is by no means self-evident. Consider, for example, Saba Mahmood's trenchant critique of secularism:

> [Modern secularism] entails fundamental shifts in conceptions of self, time, space, ethics, and morality, as well as a reorganization of social, political, and religious life. The secular, in other words, is not the natural bedrock from which religion emerges, nor is it what remains when religion is taken away. Instead, it itself is a historical product with specific epistemological, political, and moral entailments—none of which can be adequately grasped through a nominal account of secularism as the modern state's retreat from religion.[9]

Secularism, for all its claims to neutrality, has the effect of entrenching Western cultural and political formation within its spaces.[10] Religious studies as a discipline is predicated on the cultural shift toward secularism, which at first glance might seem to offer a neutral position for the engagement of religious traditions. However, as Talal Asad and Saba Mahmood have each argued, behind this historical shift from religious to secular, a variety of political changes have had to take place, which are very much invested in specific (i.e., Western) political formations. Mahmood puts it this way:

> By political secularism, following Talal Asad, I do not simply mean the principle of state neutrality toward religion but the sovereign prerogative of the state to regulate religious life through a variety of disciplinary practices that are political as well as ethical. Importantly, these disciplines of subjectivity are undertaken not simply by state but also by nonstate (civic and cultural) institutions that authorize normative models of practice, behavior, and religiosity.[11]

One of the chief authorities that helps both to define and to discipline religious practices is the scholarly study of religion itself, for it often sets the terms of what "counts" as religion, which beliefs and practices are intrinsic to it, and what sorts of religious beliefs or practices might be considered outside its range. As David Chidester has argued, the study of religion is itself a colonial project: one that seeks to demarcate things such as religious and secular, sacred and profane, holy and ordinary time, and often according to the implicit logic of Western/Christian understandings of these terms, even while religious studies claims to be divested from religious commitment. Indeed, for Chidester, "the very word *religion* must also be a focus of critical research interrogating the term's colonial productions and deployments against the background of its imperial aspirations."[12]

As a discipline, religious studies has a curiously intolerant position on theology, viewing religious belief and commitment as a delegitimating factor for scholarly enquiry, as though belief and commitment are absent from religious studies itself. While the colonial roots of Christian theology are deep and far reaching, theology, especially in its current chastened state, may be more hospitable to deep encounter with religious others. This is so because theology is predicated both upon the recognition of communal formation and the potential interruption or overthrowing of its own certainty through encounter with the other. Theology begins in the middle of formation, even while it calls such formation and the self within it ever into question.[13]

When I entered theological studies, I could scarce describe the difference between theology and religious studies, although I preferred the former intuitively. As a student, I had a vague sense that I wanted to study Augustine or Teresa of Avila as people of faith. If I were to describe my aspirations today, they would involve understanding Augustine or Teresa within the complex sociopolitical, but also spiritual, world to which they belonged—the two being intrinsically related—and to understanding the formation, practices, and dispositions that rounded out their doctrinal commitments. Talal Asad puts it this way:

> If religious symbols are understood, on the analogy with words, as vehicles for meaning, can such meanings be established independently of the form of life in which they are used? If religious symbols are to be taken as the signatures of a sacred text, can we know what they mean without regard to the social disciplines by which their correct reading is secured? If religious symbols are to be thought of as the concepts by which experiences are organized, can we say much about them without considering how they come to be authorized?[14]

Of course, Asad is an anthropologist, not a theologian. Yet he also refuses to understand religions through foundational concepts such as "religious symbols." He directs us instead to understanding religion as a complex form of life—one in which symbol and meaning, texts and practices, and individual assent and authority are intricately related. Theology as a discipline, with its complex interlocking fields of scriptural studies, history, languages, pastoral, and liturgical studies, seems to be particularly adept at understanding the complex and irreducible system that is a religious tradition in a similar way. What theology has historically lacked—and what Asad rightly points it to—is scholarly concern with "how [religious concepts] come to be authorized." This question of authority is the precise reason why theology needs feminism.

Strike Two: Feminism

Feminism shares with theology an investment in embedded or situated knowledge. Epistemologically, it holds that knowledge, by its very nature, is contingent and socially located. Like theology, it recognizes that knowledge is not simply private, but that it is socially and communally formed, and thus it safeguards the particularity of discrete subject positions. As Lorraine Code writes,

> Here *situated knowledge* does not just announce "where it (or its articulator) are coming from": it engages critically with the detail of knowledge-making situations populated by particular, fallible human beings. Such sites may be analogically ecologically interconnected, but readings insensitive to their local specificities cannot be applied whole, as though any location could stand in for any other. Meanwhile the negotiated aspect of situated knowledge ensures that its self-scrutiny reduces neither to monologic speculation nor to individualistic retreat into autobiography.[15]

Yet as Code also describes, situated knowledge is inherently critical knowledge, for it arises from subjects that have to negotiate their positionality within contexts that are often hostile to them. In a sense, this critical posture within one's situatedness is a first principle of feminist theology. It is faith seeking understanding when faith is antagonistic to women's (and other marginalized persons') self-understanding. Rosemary Radford Ruether offers a concrete illustration:

> The male bias of Jewish and Christian theology not only affects the teaching about woman's person, nature and role, but also generates a symbolic universe based on the patriarchal hierarchy of male over female. The subordination of women to man is replicated in the symbolic university in the imagery of divine-human relations. God is imaged as a great patriarch over and against the earth or Creation, imaged in female terms. Likewise Christ is related to the Church as bridegroom to bride. Divine-human relations in the macrocosm are also reflected in the microcosm of the human being. Mind over body, reason over the passions, are also seen as images of the hierarchy of the "masculine" over the "feminine." Thus everywhere the Christian and the Jew are surrounded by

religious symbols that ratify male domination and female subordination as the normative way of understanding the world and God.[16]

Gender thus gets inscribed and reinscribed within religious symbolism and texts in ways that run counter to women's flourishing. Androcentric bias creates a stark and hierarchized ordering of God and creation, man and woman, mind and body. For Ruether, one of the chief tasks of a critical feminist theology is to challenge and undermine such dualisms and propose "a useable past"—which might better serve women and other strangers within faith communities. This is critical work, but the critique is immanent to the religion itself. It thus reaffirms a situated epistemology, but it arises from a vantage of critical reflection upon one's situatedness, a vantage that is afforded by in some sense being an "outsider" within a tradition. Thus feminist theology (together with decolonial, liberationist, Queer, Black theologies, and others) make empty the claim of Hughes and other religionists for whom theology is merely a form of apologetics, "caught up in catechesis, exclusion, bigotry, and, ultimately, the creation of often elaborate discourses for constructing self and other."[17]

It is a strange perspective that views a discipline as complex and demanding as theology as parochial. As anybody remotely familiar with the discipline can attest, theology demands formidable training: linguistic, textual, philosophical, and historical, to name a few. Critical theologies such as feminist theology expand the curriculum to include economics, political and other social sciences, critical race and cultural studies. Feminist theology combines the insights of feminist theory with the experiential dimension of living within the confines and structures of the religion, while it also seeks to interrogate and transcend those confines. This twofold nature of feminist theology—as both explanatory and visionary—aligns very closely with what Sara Ahmed (following Audre Lorde) has called "sweaty concepts." Sweaty concepts as descriptors are "ways of understanding worlds that are in the worlds *we are in*"[18] (italics mine), as opposed to the worlds we observe at a distance. Christian feminist theology seeks to understand women's positionality within the form of life/world that is the church and all the vast array of habits, traditions, rituals, texts, traditions, and idiosyncrasies therein. Sweaty concepts also seek to understand women's positionality within a world that renders them an outsider, a body that is not at home in the world, while it also refuses to capitulate to the demands of that world. Sweaty concepts are thus resistant to assimilation and rub against the grain of the world into which subjects are inscribed:

> A "sweaty concept" might be one that comes out of a bodily experience that is difficult, one that is "trying," and where the aim is to keep exploring and exposing this difficulty, which means also aiming not to eliminate the effort or labour from the writing (I suspect not eliminating the effort or labour becomes an academic aim because we have been taught to tidy our texts, not to reveal the struggle we have in getting somewhere).[19]

Strike Three: Sweat

In my own religious tradition (Anglicanism), a previous generation of women came up against a multitude of trying and ridiculous arguments against their inclusion within the priesthood. One especially offensive position sought to block women from eucharistic presidency due to their messy bodily perturbances, which threatened to contaminate the sacred rite. Academia has its own methods of barring sweat and other bodily secretions from its sanctuaries. Academia is predicated upon the erasure of conceptual and bodily struggle. It asserts instead, as through an act of faith, the fantasy that our ideas are divested from partiality, struggle, and particularity. The chair to whom I appealed for work over twenty years ago was no doubt disturbed by my all too evident struggle to contain myself as a scholar—by my pregnancy, by my academic commitments that were too leaky, too porous, too obtrusive, and by my need for a job in a system from which I was being continually rendered abject.

I am happy to report that a few years after that encounter, I was hired on tenure track at another public university in a faculty of theology. As fate and circumstances would have it, that faculty would close its doors a decade later. Due to the good fortune of having tenure, however, I was able to transition smoothly to a department of religion, where I remain to this day. I still struggle with my

"Two Strikes"

sweatiness there—concealing my priestly identity, reinventing myself as "professor of Christian Thought," and assiduously translating my public grant proposals into the official Esperanto of Canadian multicultural pluralism. Writing for *Women in Theology* is a relief for me because I can be unapologetically sweaty for this blog. It is here that I can work on all those messy and porous themes that recognize we are embodied beings who struggle—struggle with our religious traditions and with the wider world in which sexism, racism, homophobia, ableism, and climate catastrophe surround and threaten us daily. I write for *Women in Theology* because I believe that religion and the wider culture are inextricably bound and that the separation of the two is always a fraught and a political practice. I write for *Women in Theology* because I do not think that belief or bodies can be extricated from scholarly work. Nor should they. In a world teetering on catastrophe, we can no longer hope that our deepest desires, aspirations, and commitments can be represented by putatively objective and abstract reason.

I also write for *Women in Theology* because I am inspired by the badassery of younger theologians for whom the old strictures and separations seem not to apply. These are women, BIPoC, and LGBTQ+ folk who have said no to the myth of conceptual purity. Such younger feminist theologians are not intimidated by crossing borders into other disciplines. They also refuse to believe that the church has some special revelation that makes it impervious to radical critique and yet they wish to engage with it and to engage within it. I write for *Women in Theology* because I am surrounded there by the sweaty conceptual labor of authors and allies who understand that the struggle for knowledge must be intimately tied to the struggle of women and other marginalized groups, of this fragile planet and its creatures. And so, I draw inspiration from a younger generation of feminist theologians for whom such sweaty concepts are second nature, and I hope that it makes me bolder in my own scholarly endeavors.

And so, to them and to all the younger feminist theologians who read the blog: thank you. I hope that you never have to deal with Professor Two Strikes, but if you do, I hope you know that you have already smashed that ball out of the whole ridiculous park.

NOTES

1. This essay was originally published, in briefer form, as Jane Barter "'Two Strikes': Why I Write for 'Women in Theology,'" *WIT: Women in Theology*, August 25, 2019, https://womenintheology.org/2019/08/25/two-strikes-why-i-write-for-women-in-theology/.

2. See E. R. Forbes, "Epilogue: The 1980s," in *The Atlantic Provinces in Confederation*, ed. E. R. Forbes and D. A. Muise (Toronto: University of Toronto Press, 2016), 505–16.

3. Robert Laxer, *The Liberal Idea of Canada: Pierre Trudeau and the Question of Canada's Survival* (Toronto: James Lorimer and Company, 1977).

4. Brian Clarke and Stuart Macdonald, *Leaving Christianity: Changing Allegiances in Canada since 1945* (Montreal: McGill-Queen's Press, 2017), 6.

5. D. Haskall Millard, Stephanie Burgoyne, and Kevin N. Flatt, "Mainline Denominational Switching in Canada: Comparing the Religious Trajectories of Growing and Declining Church Attendees," *The Canadian Journal of Sociology / Cahiers Canadiens de Sociologie* 41, no. 4 (2016): 494.

6. Aaron Hughes, *From Seminary to University: An Institutional History of the Study of Religion in Canada* (Toronto: University of Toronto Press, 2020), 137.

7. Hughes, *From Seminary to University*, 6.

8. For an exploration of the coercive underside to national strategies aimed at multiculturalism, see Wendy Brown, *Regulating Aversion: Tolerance in the Age of Identity and Empire* (Princeton, NJ: Woodstock, 2008). For a specifically Indigenous response to Canada's deployment of multicultural politics, see May Chazan, *Home and Native Land: Unsettling Multiculturalism in Canada* (Toronto: Between the Lines, 2011).

9. Saba Mahmood, "Introduction," in *Religious Difference in a Secular Age: A Minority Report* (Princeton, NJ: Princeton University Press, 2016), 3.

10. Talal Asad, *Formations of the Secular* (Stanford, CA: Stanford University Press, 2003).

11. Saba Mahmood, "Can Secularism Be Other-Wise?" in *Varieties of Secularism in a Secular Age*, ed. Michael Warner, Jonathan

Vanandtwerpen, and Craig Calhoun (Cambridge, MA: Harvard University Press, 2010), 293.

12. David Chidester, *Religion: Material Dynamics* (Oakland: University of California Press, 2018), 122.

13. Here, I think of the work of such scholars as Joshua Ralston in Islamic-Christian comparative theology, or the long-standing efforts of David Burrell, Francis Clooney, and Catherine Cornille.

14. Talal Asad, "The Construction of Religion as an Anthropological Category," in *Genealogies of Religion* (Baltimore: Johns Hopkins University Press, 1993), 128.

15. Lorraine Code, "Feminist Epistemologies and Women's Lives," in *The Blackwell Guide to Feminist Philosophy*, ed. Linda Martin Alcoff and Eva Feder Kittay (Hoboken, NJ: Wiley, 2006), 230.

16. Rosemary Radford Ruether, "The Feminist Critique in Religious Studies," *Soundings: An Interdisciplinary Journal* 64, no. 4 (1981): 390.

17. Hughes, *From Seminary to University*, 175.

18. Sara Ahmed, "Sweaty Concepts," https://feministkilljoys.com/2014/02/22/sweaty-concepts.

19. Ahmed, "Sweaty Concepts."

CONTRIBUTORS

Alexandria Barbera (she/her) lives in Ontario, Canada and joined *Women in Theology* as a regular contributor in 2016. She is a freelance writer and editor who holds degrees from Queen's University, McMaster Divinity College, and Trent University. Her graduate research has focused on origin theories of literary texts, biblical theologies of inspiration, and literary ecology. She was the managing editor at *EcoTheo Review* from 2018 to 2021 . Her writing and poetry have appeared in *The Other Journal, Ekstasis Magazine, Amethyst Review,* and several prominent haiku journals throughout Canada, Britain, and the United States. She is an ardent supporter of gender equality and women's inclusion in all areas of life.

Jane Barter (she/her) is professor in the Department of Religion and Culture, The University of Winnipeg. She holds a PhD in theology from the University of Saint Michael's College, University of Toronto. She is author of two monographs in Theology: *Lord, Giver of Life* (Wilfrid Laurier University Press) and *Thinking Christ* (Fortress Press). She is currently editing the Christology volume for *The Bloomsbury Encyclopaedia of Christian Theology*. She also writes in the areas of feminist theory and settler colonial studies. She was a regular contributor to *Women in Theology* from 2016 to 2022, contributing many essays at the crossroads of theology and culture.

Elissa Cutter (she/her) is a feminist historical theologian whose research contributes to efforts to recover women's voices in the history of Christianity as theologians. In particular, she is in the progress of articulating an explicit methodology for feminist historical theology. She presently does this through the lens of the nuns of the convent of Port-Royal in seventeenth-century France. She received her PhD in theological studies, with a focus on historical theology and modern Christianity, from Saint Louis University. She is currently assistant professor of religious studies and theology at Georgian Court University, a Mercy institution in New Jersey. There, she regularly teaches courses about the Christian tradition, ethics, Catholic social teaching, and theological method. She has blogged with *Women in Theology* since 2013 and took on the role of coeditor with Allison Murray in 2018.

Brandy Daniels (she/her) is an assistant professor of theology and gender and women's studies at the University of Portland. She has a PhD in religion and gender studies from Vanderbilt University and an MDiv and MA in comparative literature and African American Studies from Duke University. Standing at the intersections of constructive and political theologies, social ethics, and feminist and queer theories, Brandy's scholarship explores the place of difference within communal identity and belonging, focusing particularly on gender and sexual difference in Christian thought and practice. She is working on her first monograph, entitled *How (Not) to Be Christian*. Brandy cochairs the Queer Studies in Religion unit of the American Academy of Religion, the LGBTQIA+ Working Group of the Society for Christian Ethics, and is on the executive committee for the Political Theology Network. She is an ordained Disciples of Christ minister and a part of Portland Interfaith Clergy Resistance. Brandy wrote for *Women in Theology* from 2013 to 2015.

Jessica Gapasin Dennis (she/her) writes from the perspective of a second-generation Filipina American and holds an MA in pastoral studies from the Washington Theological Union with background theology coursework from the Franciscan University of Steubenville. Her current areas of research include the interpretation of Scripture through a decolonized lens and children's catechesis. Jessica lives in the Washington, DC, metro area with her husband and two girls and has been a regular contributor for *Women in Theology* since 2018.

Contributors

Maria Gwyn McDowell (she/her) is a priest in the Episcopal Church, a teacher, and public theologian in love with the God who calls all to liberation and compassion. She is committed to working and playing alongside God in communities seeking to practice justice, mercy, and joy in our world. She blogs at *DeiProfundis* (https://deiprofundis.org/), and has contributed to *Women in Theology* since 2013. She received her PhD in theological ethics from Boston College, where she wrote on gender, sexuality, and women through the lens of virtue and liberation ethics. She continues to learn and grow in her feminist and antiracist commitments as the rector of Episcopal parishes in the Pacific Northwest. You may find her work at http://mariagwyn.com.

Janice McRandal (she/her) is a feminist theologian who works as the director of the cooperative, a center for public theology in Brisbane, Australia. Her publications include *Christian Doctrine and the Grammar of Difference: A Contribution to Feminist Systematic Theology* and *Sarah Coakley and the Future of Systematic Theology*. Janice has a PhD in systematic theology and her current research explores political theology and sport in relation to traditional Christian doctrine. She answered a call to join the *Women in Theology* blog in 2013 because, after five years of postgraduate theological study in Australia, she had not met a single person studying feminist theology, and was a regular contributor until 2015.

Caroline Morris (she/they) is a hospice chaplain. She has studied anorexia and its relationship to Christianity and asceticism for many years. Caroline wrote a thesis titled "The Anorexic's Anorexia" when she was first beginning to explore the connections between anorexia and asceticism, spirituality, fasting, and chastity in church history and Western evangelical dieting culture. Caroline has a BA in English literature and graduated from Earlham School of Religion (ESR) with a master of divinity degree in 2020. Caroline was the recipient of ESR's 2019 Mullen Ministry of Writing Fellowship and has been writing for *Women in Theology* since 2018.

Allison Murray (she/her) is a historian of Christianity with a PhD in theological studies from the University of Toronto (Emmanuel

College, 2021). Her previous studies earned her an MTS from Conrad Grebel University College at the University of Waterloo and a BA in Religion and Culture and History from Wilfrid Laurier University. Her primary field of research is the history of theological ideas about gender and their social, political, and institutional implications over time. Her dissertation "Building Biblical Manhood and Womanhood: White American Evangelical Complementarianism, 1970–2010" focused on theologies of gender in evangelical trade publications. She is currently a sessional lecturer at the University of Waterloo and teaching religious studies, philosophy, and history at the secondary level. Allison joined *Women in Theology* as a regular contributor in 2016 and has been serving as coeditor of the blog since 2018.

Mandy Rodgers-Gates (she/her) completed MTS and ThM degrees at Duke University, with a thesis titled "Dying to Point the Way to Life: The Political Power of Oscar Romero's Solidarity with Christ, the Poor, and the Church." Her current work includes the spiritual and theological formation of teenagers, as well as the effects of Christian nationalism on white evangelical churches. She was a regular contributor to *Women in Theology* from 2016 to 2021.

www.ingramcontent.com/pod-product-compliance
Lightning Source LLC
Chambersburg PA
CBHW070944230426
43666CB00011B/2550